INTRODUCTION
TO
GARDENING

INTRODUCTION
TO
GARDENING

Peter McHoy

Abbeydale Press

This edition first published by Abbeydale Press
an imprint of Bookmart Limited
Desford Road, Enderby,
Leicestershire LE9 5AD
United Kingdom

© Bookmart Limited 1996

ISBN 1-86147-004-5

Editorial Director Joanna Lorenz
Project Editor Jennifer Jones
Assistant Editor Sarah Ainley
Photographer Paul Forrester
Designer Michael Morey
Illustrator Kate Simunek

Typeset by MC Typeset Limited

Printed in Singapore by Star Standard Industries Pte. Ltd.

Previously published as part of a larger compendium,
The Practical Gardening Encyclopedia.

CONTENTS

Introduction 7

Choosing tools 1: Digging and
    cultivating tools 12

Choosing tools 2: Mowers 14

Choosing tools 3: Trimming and
    pruning tools 16

Choosing tools 4: Other useful tools 18

Preparing the ground 1 20

Preparing the ground 2 22

Testing your soil 24

Improving your soil 26

Making garden compost 28

Fertilizers and manures 1 30

Fertilizers and manures 2 32

Watering 34

Weeding beds and borders 36

Weeding lawns and paths 38

Pest control 1: Aphids and other
    sap-suckers 40

Pest control 2: Leaf-eaters 41

Pest control 3: Root-eaters 42

Disease control 1: Leaf diseases 43

Disease control 2: Root diseases 44

Physiological and other problems 45

Sowing in pots and trays 46

Pricking out 48

Sowing hardy annuals 50

Sowing alpines and shrubs 52

Softwood and greenwood cuttings 54

Basal stem cuttings 56

Semi-ripe cuttings 58

Special cuttings 60

Hardwood cuttings 62

Layering 64

Leaf cuttings 66

Division 68

Root cuttings 70

Pruning 1 72

Pruning 2 74

Pruning 3 76

Rustic arches and pergolas 78

Fences 80

Walls 82

Surfaces and paths 1 84

Surfaces and paths 2 86

Surfaces and paths 3 88

Edgings 90

Suppliers 92

Index 94

INTRODUCTION

Gardening is an enormously rewarding activity. Besides providing decoration to enhance the home, it is the perfect way to escape the stresses of modern life and get back in touch with the tranquility and rhythms of nature.

The pleasure we derive from gardening comes as much from the way in which we create our beautiful gardens as it does from the final result. The routine care needed to achieve displays of foliage and colour teaches much about our garden's needs, and by responding to these needs with the most effective treatments, we will ensure ourselves the best results. Ultimately, better results will mean greater satisfaction and a more beautiful place to relax in.

OPPOSITE
Be flexible in the way you approach your planting. In this border there is a happy mixture of annuals and shrubby plants together with the herbaceous plants.

A garden does not look after itself, and if you want to get the best from your plants you have to think about the basics like watering, feeding, weeding, and pest and disease control. Fortunately, as the following pages show, these need not become onerous chores . . . and they are well offset by the delights to be discovered in the more 'creative' aspects of gardening such as propagation. Even pruning can be creative, as you learn to shape the shrubs as well as improve their flowering.

OPPOSITE
Propagation is one of the most satisfying aspects of gardening, and if you have a greenhouse the scope is widened enormously.

Gardening is a practical hobby that combines the art of design and the creative use of plants with the science of horticulture and the mechanics of garden construction. The following pages will help you to build a better garden and to keep your plants growing healthily.

Using the right tools always makes gardening easier, and whether you are just beginning to garden or have been growing plants for years and simply want to replace an old tool, the advice on choosing tools will get you off to a good start.

Adequate ground preparation is something that beginners in particular overlook, yet it can spell the difference between success and failure. In the following pages you will find hints and tips on testing and improving your soil, and advice on how to make good garden

ABOVE A weed-free lawn is as easy as watering, if you use one of the modern selective hormone weedkillers.

compost . . . something that even experienced gardeners can find difficult to achieve.

Few plants will thrive without feeding and watering, and there are plenty of practical know-how tips to take the mystique and hard work out of both chores.

Pests and other problems are part of gardening. Even the most expert gardener gets them. You will find simple no-nonsense advice on how to deal with some of the most common problems, with an organic solution as well as a chemical approach wherever appropriate.

Propagation is not only money-saving, it's fun and very satisfying. You will find all the major propagation techniques described in easy-to-follow steps, with a section on special or unusual techniques for those who like to try something a little different.

ABOVE Even paving stone paths can be interesting if you use your imagination and mix materials. Here, beach pebbles are being used to vary the texture.

LEFT Hand weeding still has a place, especially close to other plants.

LEFT A sawn log path, surrounded by chipped bark, makes an attractive path for a wild part of the garden.

BELOW Lawns benefit from a neat, crisp edge, and proprietary lawn edging strips do the job well.

Pruning is perhaps the one task that newcomers — and even many experienced gardeners — tackle with the most trepidation. The section on pruning removes the mystique by reducing the problem to a few common-sense steps that will cover the majority of shrubs.

Whether you are starting a garden from scratch or adding to an existing one, perhaps by building a patio or pergola, some construction work is inevitable. Even if you are a newcomer to it, you will find here all the information you need for basic garden construction jobs.

ABOVE, CENTRE Keep on top of pests and diseases, especially with plants prone to them, such as roses.

ABOVE Propagation can be as simple as pegging down a shoot on those plants that can be layered.

LEFT Routine pruning will keep shrubs such as roses in good shape and flowering well.

GARDENING BASICS

11

CHOOSING TOOLS 1:
DIGGING AND CULTIVATING TOOLS

The right tools really do make a difference. A good quality, well-designed tool will often make a job much easier and will help to take the hard work out of gardening.

SPADES

Choose a spade with a long handle if you are tall. If you can afford it, a stainless steel spade will make digging easier.

■ A D-shaped hilt provides a good grip – but make sure that you can get your hand in easily when wearing a gardening glove.

■ Choose a full-sized blade if you have a lot of digging to do, but if you want a spade only to cultivate established borders or to plant trees and shrubs, a border spade with a blade of about 23 × 13cm (9 × 5in) may be more useful.

■ A tread on top of the blade makes it less tiring on the feet when you push the spade into the ground, but the spade will be a little heavier as a result. Stainless steel spades do not have treads.

■ A wooden shaft is strong and comfortable to hold. Metal shafts should be coated with plastic.

Left: special trowel designed to fit onto separate handle as part of a range of tools. Centre: traditional hand trowel and fork. Right: narrow trowel, useful for a rock garden

FORKS

A garden fork can be used instead of a spade for digging on heavy clay soils, but it is also invaluable for lifting bulky material such as manure and garden compost.

■ A D-shaped hilt is generally stronger than a Y-shaped one, and more widely available than T-shaped hilts. Make sure that you can fit your hand in easily when wearing a gardening glove.

■ For general cultivation and lifting, choose a full-sized head with square prongs.

HOES AND RAKES

A hoe is one of the basic gardening tools, vital if you want to keep down the weeds. If you want one hoe, go for the Dutch type.

■ The Dutch hoe is excellent for weeding between rows and around plants. Its angled head is designed to slice through weeds with the

Left: weeding trowel. Centre: patio/paving weeder. Right: daisy grubber

Spade

Fork

GARDENING BASICS

Left: draw hoe. Centre: proprietary three-bladed hoe. Right: Dutch hoe

minimum damage to plant roots. The wider the head, the quicker the weeding, but a narrow head is easier to use among plants.

■ Choose a long handle so that you have less bending to do.

■ An angled end and moulded grip make the tool easier to use.

■ A draw hoe has an angled head that is useful for taking out flat-bottomed drills for seeds (use the corner for a normal drill), and for drawing up earth around crops such as potatoes. You can also use it to weed with a chopping motion.

■ Patent hoe designs sometimes have a smaller blade that cuts on more than one side for working close in among plants.

A rake is most useful in a kitchen garden where you need to level the soil regularly, and when making a new garden.

■ Choose a long handle so that you have less bending to do.

■ Buy a head that is made in one piece. Riveted heads are not so strong. The wider the head, the more quickly you can rake an area, but balance this against the extra weight involved.

HAND CULTIVATORS AND WEEDERS

Hand cultivators are useful for breaking up the ground after digging, and for weeding between and along rows of seedlings or small plants, but are less efficient than a hoe for this task.

■ A cultivator that has removable prongs is more versatile than a fixed-prong type, especially when working among plants.

■ Choose one with a long handle. A handle that can be used with other heads and accessories is useful.

Special tools are available for grubbing out daisies and other weeds in a lawn, and others are designed for weeding among paving. These are useful, but worth buying only if you have a regular use for them.

Hand cultivator head that can be fitted to a long or short proprietary handle

HAND FORKS AND TROWELS

Trowels are inexpensive and indispensable – you will need them for planting, but they are also useful for weeding and filling pots and containers with compost.

You can manage without a hand fork, but it is useful for weeding and loosening soil.

■ A wide-bladed trowel is best for planting and general use around the garden. A stainless steel blade is well worth the extra money you will pay, as it will not rust and should last much longer.

■ A narrow blade is useful for working in confined areas, such as a rock garden.

■ When buying a hand fork, make sure that the prongs are strong and the head is firmly fixed to the handle part.

Left: conventional rake. Above: a proprietary rake design

Hand weeder, also called a hand grubber

Choosing Tools 2: Mowers

Almost every gardener owns a mower, but it is important to choose the most appropriate type for your garden.

Which Mower?

Manual mowers are worth considering for a very small lawn.

Side-wheel mowers without a roller attachment are the lightest and easiest to use.

Rear-roller mowers are the best choice for a small lawn if you want a striped finish.

Wheeled rotary electric mowers are the first choice for a lawn of modest size if you do not require a striped finish. For a large lawn, where trailing cables could be a problem, a petrol cylinder mower is a better and safer choice.

Hover rotary mowers – electric or petrol – are useful for cutting awkward places, such as beneath low overhanging branches, and shallow slopes. They are light and easy to manoeuvre.

Although rotary mowers do not usually have rear rollers to produce stripes or grass boxes to collect grass, this is not always the case – models are available that have both of these features. Shop around to see what is available at the time you want to buy.

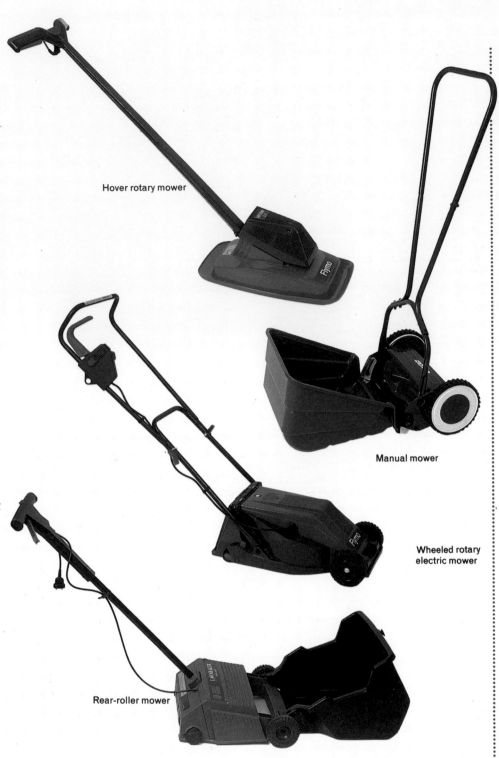

Hover rotary mower

Manual mower

Wheeled rotary electric mower

Rear-roller mower

Sharpening

You can sharpen mower blades yourself, especially those of rotary mowers, but it is best to have them done professionally. Rotary mower blades are not expensive to replace. Some models can be fitted with plastic safety blades, and you may want to consider using these.

Electrical Safety

Check the cables and plugs on electric mowers for damage or loose connections. Always do this at the beginning of each season, but do not be complacent between-times. If your house wiring is not fitted with an earth leakage circuit breaker (or residual current device), buy a special power point which has one fitted. You can then use it for all your electrical gardening equipment.

Always brush or wipe the blades clean after mowing. Remove any accumulations of mowings noticed on other parts of the mower. *Always disconnect the power supply before cleaning an electric mower*.

Adjust the cutting height periodically to suit the time of year and rate of growth of the grass. Cut high in the spring, and then gradually reduce the height. The adjustments on your cylinder mower may

not be the same as the mower illustrated – consult the manufacturer's handbook. Rotary mowers can also be adjusted for height of cut. Consult the manufacturer's manual for the correct method.

Adjust the blades of a cylinder mower so that it cuts cleanly and evenly along the length of the blade. Use a sheet of paper to check that it cuts cleanly along the length of the blade. Rotate the cylinder slowly and carefully as you move the sheet of paper along the length of the cylinder.

If the paper does not cut cleanly along the length of the blade, make the necessary adjustment to the blade setting. Your mower may work on a different principle, so consult the handbook for your particular machine.

At the beginning of the season, and every month or two afterwards, put a drop of oil on bearings and chains. This will make the mower much easier to push.

WINTER WORK

Drain the petrol and oil from a petrol mower before you put it away for the winter.

Clean and adjust or replace the spark plug. Check your handbook for the appropriate gap setting.

Before replacing the spark plug, pour a tablespoonful of oil into the cylinder. Then pull the starter to turn the engine over about half a dozen times before replacing the spark plug.

Wipe the mower with an oily rag, or spray with an anti-rust aerosol, before storing.

Before storing a rotary petrol or electric mower, clean the metal blades with an emery cloth.

Wipe the blade over with an oily rag to reduce the risk of rusting. If the blade is in poor condition, replace it with a new one.

CHOOSING TOOLS 3: TRIMMING AND PRUNING TOOLS

After cutting the lawn, hedge-trimming is one of the most labour-intensive and boring jobs in the garden. Electric hedge-trimmers make light work of the task, but hand shears may be preferable for a short hedge or trimming an individual shrub.

HEDGE-TRIMMERS

The longer the cutting length of a hedge-trimmer, the more quickly you will cut the hedge. The longest blades are usually found on heavy machines, however, and petrol-powered hedge-trimmers in particular are tiring to use. A 40cm (16in) blade is suitable for a small or medium-sized garden, but if you have a large garden with a lot of hedges, a 60cm (24in) blade will save a lot of time.

■ A double-sided cutting edge is useful if you like to cut with a sweep in both directions, but many gardeners use hedge-trimmers with a sweep in one direction only.

■ If both blades move (rather than one moving blade cutting against a stationary blade), vibration is likely to be much less. This is called a reciprocating action.

Hand shears

■ The more teeth there are for a given length of blade, the finer the finish is likely to be – but widely spaced teeth cope better with very thick shoots.

■ Blade extensions that project beyond the cutting blades reduce the risk of injury. These are also described as blade guards.

■ A hand shield should always be included with the hedge-trimmer.

■ A lock-off switch, which requires two separate actions to turn on the machine, makes accidental starting less likely.

CHOOSING HAND SHEARS

Hand shears, also called hedging shears, must be kept sharp, and the pivots or bearings oiled regularly to reduce the amount of physical effort required.

■ Make sure that the blades are easy to adjust. If too slack they will not cut properly; if too tight they will be hard to use.

■ Most shears have straight blades. These with wavy blades tend to cut through hard shoots more easily, but sharpening them is difficult.

■ A thick-shoot notch in the blade is useful if you have to cut through

Hedge-trimmer
with double cutting
edge and blade
guards

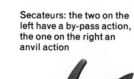

SECATEURS

■ Anvil secateurs cut when a sharp blade slicing through the stem is held against a flat anvil (usually made of a softer material). The anvil sometimes has a groove in it to allow the sap to run away. Anvil secateurs are likely to crush or tear the stem if the blade is not kept well sharpened.

■ By-pass secateurs have a scissor-like action, and are more likely to produce a sharp, clean cut than anvil secateurs.

■ Brightly coloured handles make the tool easier to see if you put it down whilst working.

■ The safety catch should be convenient and easy to use.

■ Make sure that the spring does not hold the blades open too wide or offer too much resistance to allow for a comfortable grip.

Secateurs: the two on the left have a by-pass action, the one on the right an anvil action

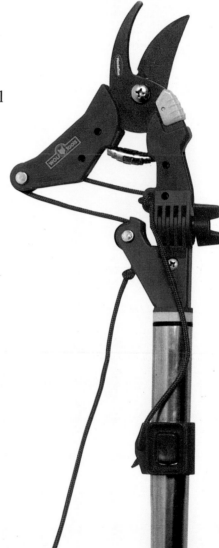

LONG-HANDLED PRUNERS

You will find these sold under a variety of names, such as loppers and branch cutters, but they all do the same job: cut through shoots and branches too thick for ordinary secateurs, and make reaching within a shrub much easier.

■ By-pass blades may be easier to manoeuvre into a confined space.

■ The longer the handle, the more leverage you will have and the less effort required to cut through a thick branch.

Long-handled pruners, sometimes called loppers

a thick shoot and you don't have secateurs to hand.

■ Handles are less important than the blades. Their shape and the material they are made from have little bearing on the ease with which the shears are used.

Tree pruner

CHOOSING TOOLS 4: OTHER USEFUL TOOLS

As well as the traditional garden tools there are newer ones designed to do specific jobs, such as shredding garden waste or raking moss from lawns. Some of the most useful ones are described here.

NYLON-LINE TRIMMERS
Nylon-line trimmers are the modern equivalent of the traditional scythe, but they are far more versatile and useful.

Electric shredder

Use them to trim long grass around trees or right up to the edge of a fence or wall (difficult to do with a mower), or for chopping down weeds. More powerful machines with stronger cutters (sometimes metal discs) are called brushwood cutters; these are suitable for tough undergrowth.

▌ A cutting guide will keep the spinning line off the ground and prevent it scalping the ground.
▌ Two handles are needed to control a trimmer easily, and an adjustable shaft handle makes manoeuvring easier.
▌ An automatic or semi-automatic line feed is useful as the line soon wears away.
▌ A swivel head is useful if you want to use the trimmer to edge a lawn. It's easier than trying to hold the whole tool at an angle.

SHREDDERS
Shredders are useful if you like to recycle as much garden refuse as possible, but their cost is usually justified only if you have a lot of material to shred.

Shredders chop or mash woody and soft material so that it rots down more easily on the compost heap.

▌ The outlet spout should be high enough off the ground to slide containers beneath it easily. Sack holder clips are useful for collecting material in sacks.

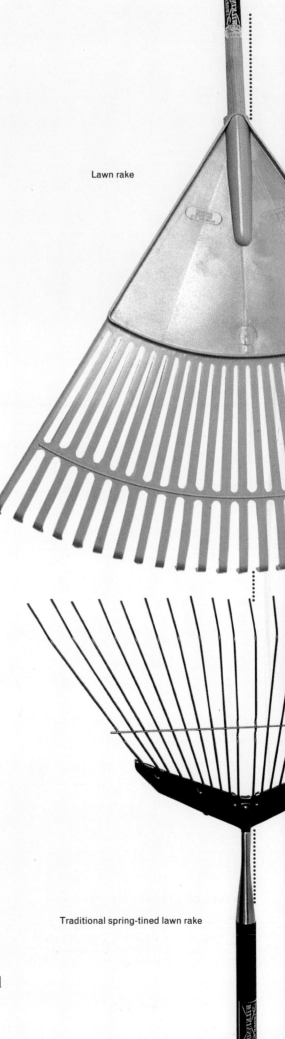

Lawn rake

Traditional spring-tined lawn rake

GARDENING BASICS

■ The inlet funnel should be large enough to use easily – but you should not be able to touch any moving parts.

■ Wheels are very useful. Shredders are heavy, and electric shredders cannot be left outside unprotected. One without wheels is satisfactory if you are able to use it where it is stored, but make sure that the legs are sturdy and stable.

LAWN RAKES

Lawn rakes are useful for raking out moss and 'thatch' (the dead grass and debris that forms around the base of the grass plants) from a lawn. They are also useful for scattering worm casts and raking up autumn leaves.

■ There are many kinds of manual lawn rakes, but the traditional fan-shaped spring-tined rake is one of the most useful. It is light and easy to use, and works well.

■ Powered lawn rakes save a lot of effort if you have a large lawn. They also have the benefit of collecting the leaves, moss and general debris as you work.

■ The wider the machine, the more expensive it is likely to be, but for a large lawn the saving in time will make it worthwhile.

EDGING TOOLS

If you have a large lawn with a lot of edges, a half-moon edger (also called an edging iron) could be useful. It is used against a straight-edged piece of wood (one foot on the wood to steady it, the foot pressing on the tool) to straighten an uneven edge.

Although useful, over-use will gradually make your lawn smaller and beds and borders bigger!

Use long-handled edging shears or a nylon-line trimmer with a swivel head to trim grass that simply overhangs the edge.

If the edge keeps getting broken down, buy a metal or plastic edging strip to reduce the problem.

Half-moon edgers, sometimes called edging irons

Nylon line trimmer

Digging helps to aerate the soil and expose pests to predators, and gives you the chance to incorporate humus-forming manures or garden compost. For heavy clay soils it can also help to improve the structure. The autumn and early winter is the best time for digging, but you can finish it off in the spring.

SINGLE DIGGING

1 If you have a large area to dig such as a vegetable plot, or a new garden to cultivate, divide it into two equal areas. Then you can dig to one end and work back down the other side to finish where you began.

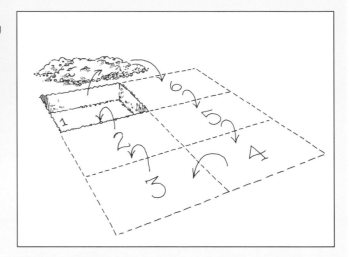

2 **ABOVE** Remove a trench the width and depth of a spade, and pile up the soil at the end of the bed.

3 **ABOVE RIGHT** Drive the spade into the soil at right angles, and no more than a spade's width away from the previous 'bite' of soil. Push the spade in as far as possible without having to kick it in.

4 **RIGHT** Push the spade in parallel to the trench, taking a bite about 15–20cm (6–8in) deep. Do not take larger bites otherwise they will be heavy to lift. If necessary use your foot to press the spade fully into the ground.

GARDENING BASICS

5 Pull back on the handle, using it as a lever to loosen the bite of soil, which will pull free on to the blade.

6 Lift the bite of soil, keeping your back as straight as possible and doing the lifting with your knees, and flick the soil over with a twist of the wrist. Inverting the clods of soil will bury the weeds. When you have reached the end of a row, work back in the opposite direction. To remove the first bite from each row, make two slices at right angles before inserting the spade between them parallel to the trench.

DIGGING A SMALL AREA

For a small area of ground in the garden, don't bother to divide the area or to remove the initial trench. Just throw the soil forward slightly as you work, then rake it level when preparing the ground for sowing or planting.

7 When you reach the end of the plot, fill the last trench with soil from the first row of the return half.

8 When you have dug the last row, fill in the trench left with the soil excavated from the first trench.

PERENNIAL WEEDS

If the soil is inverted properly, most annual weeds will be killed and will decompose to add humus to the soil. Remove the roots of troublesome perennial weeds by hand to prevent their spread.

USING A GARDEN FORK

Use a spade for normal digging, but choose a fork to loosen ground that has already been dug recently and simply needs aerating, or where persistent perennial weeds are a problem. A fork is less likely to slice through the roots to leave pieces behind, and by shaking the soil through the prongs it is easier to remove troublesome weeds.

Loosen the roots with a garden fork.

Pull up the roots by hand.

PREPARING THE GROUND 2

Whether planting or sowing seeds, you need to break the soil down to a fine tilth (structure) first after digging to open it up and remove weeds. Fine, crumbly soil is essential if you are sowing seeds, and for a lawn or an area where appearance is important, you may need to level the surface too.

PRODUCING A FINE TILTH (STRUCTURE)

1 Remove any large weeds that have been missed when digging, or that have started to grow since. Be especially careful to pull out completely the roots of pernicious weeds that grow and spread if just a few are left behind.

2 If the initial digging was done in the autumn and you are sowing or planting in the spring, go over the ground with a fork to turn in weed seedlings that have germinated, and to open up the soil again.

LEVELLING WITH PEGS

1 Prepare a supply of pegs about 15cm (6in) long. Paint or mark a band all round each peg, about 12–25mm (½–1in) from the top. It is not critical which distance you choose, but it is important that each peg is marked in exactly the same position.

2 Level the ground roughly by eye first, then insert a row of pegs about 1m (1yd) apart, using a known level surface as a reference point if possible. Push the pegs in so that the painted mark is at soil level.

3 Insert another row of pegs 1m (1yd) away from the first row. Use a long spirit-level (or a shorter one on a straight-edged piece of wood) to make sure that the pegs in each row are level. Check each peg in more than one direction, and adjust the height of the pegs as required.

4 Once each row of pegs has been levelled accurately, go on to the next row. Repeat the process until the area has been pegged. Rake the soil level, making sure that it comes up to the same position on each peg.

3 A hand cultivator like the one shown here is useful for breaking down large clods of earth and doing some of the initial levelling. Use it with a pulling motion.

4 Use an ordinary garden rake for the main levelling and smoothing, raking first in one direction and then the other.

5 You can use a combination of hoe and rake to produce a very fine soil structure for a seed bed, but a tool like this star-wheeled cultivator will make the job easier. Pushing it to and fro will break down the soil to make it fine and crumbly.

Seeds need a light, fine soil if they are to flourish.

TESTING YOUR SOIL

You can't determine how acid or alkaline your soil is, or how rich or deficient in nutrients, just by looking at it. Fortunately, simple and inexpensive soil-testing kits will give you quick results without the time or expense of a proper laboratory test. However, none of the do-it-yourself kits described here are as accurate as using a soil test laboratory, but they are better than nothing.

TESTING FOR MAJOR NUTRIENTS

1 Gather your soil sample, using a trowel, from 5–8cm (2–3in) below the surface. Take several samples from around the garden, and test each one separately.

2 Use a measure such as the lid of an aerosol can, and mix 1 part soil to 5 parts water. Shake or stir the soil and water in a clean jar, then allow it to settle – it may take anything between half an hour and a day to become reasonably clear (clay soils are the slowest).

3 Carefully draw off some clear liquid from the top few centimetres for the test.

4 Using the pipette, transfer the solution to the test and reference chambers of the plastic container.

5 Pour the powder from the capsule provided into the test chamber. Replace the cap and shake vigorously until the powder has been dispersed.

6 Wait for a few minutes for the colour to develop, then read it off against the comparison chart. There will be a key that explains the implication of each reading, and accompanying instructions will tell you how to correct any problem.

GARDENING BASICS

APPLYING LIME

1 Try not to handle lime unnecessarily – ground limestone is relatively easy and safe to handle, but hydrated lime (the form often used) is slightly caustic. Use gloves and goggles when applying it. Divide the area into 1m (1yd) squares and weigh out enough for each square (see Box for rates), then if possible apply it with a spade, sprinkling it as evenly as possible.

2 Use a rake to cover the lime and work it into the ground.

HOW MUCH LIME?

Use the following table as a guide to the amount of lime needed to raise the pH of your soil by 1 pH. It is better to make several smaller applications over time than one big dose if you need to raise the pH by much. Test the soil again after a month, and apply more lime if necessary.

Do not apply lime at the same time as manure as there may be reaction that releases nitrogen in a form that can harm nearby plants, and it is wasteful of a useful fertilizer. Try to separate applications by several months.

TYPE OF SOIL	HYDRATED LIME	GROUND LIMESTONE
CLAY	640g/sq m (18oz/sq yd)	850g/sq m (24oz/sq yd)
AVERAGE LOAM	410g/sq m (12oz/sq yd)	550g/sq m (16oz/sq yd)
SAND	200g/sq m (6oz/sq yd)	275g/sq m (8oz/sq yd)

There are chemicals that will make the soil more acid, but this is seldom a very satisfactory solution. For the ornamental garden it is best to grow plants that like the soil you already have; for vegetables the best way to make a soil more acid is to add garden compost at the rate of 9kg/sq m (20lb/sq yd) or manure at the rate of 3kg/sq m (6lb/sq yd) to raise the acidity by about 1 pH.

A HANDY TEST

If you are not sure whether your soil is sandy, a medium loam, or clay, try the following test:

▮ Pick up a handful of damp but not wet soil and try to rub it between finger and thumb. If it feels gritty but the grains do not stick together, and it is difficult to roll into a ball, it is **sandy**.
▮ If it is gritty but can be rolled into a ball, it is a **sandy loam**.
▮ If it is gritty or sticky and can be rolled into a cylinder, it is **sandy clay loam** or a **clay loam**.
▮ If you can bend the cylinder into a ring, it is **clay**.

PROBE METER

Meters are even quicker to use than indicator kits, but some people think they are less accurate. It is important to use them carefully as recommended. Keep the probe clean and, if recommended by the manufacturer, keep the tip clean with very fine emery paper.

Push the probe into the soil and after a few moments read the pH shown on the dial. Make several attempts in the same area of ground to make sure that you get a consistent reading.

TESTING THE pH

The pH test is slightly different as you don't have to wait for the mixture to settle after the soil and water have been shaken together, and only the test chamber is filled with this solution. Fill the reference chamber with clean tap water.

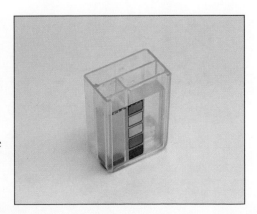

IMPROVING YOUR SOIL

All soils benefit if you can add plenty of humus-forming material such as garden compost or well-rotted manure. Clay soils can also be improved by good drainage.

CREATING A SUMP

It may be possible to drain the land into a natural drain or ditch (check whether this is permissible first), otherwise make a sump in a low part of the garden and arrange the drains so that the water flows into it. The soakaway must be at least 60cm (2ft) deep. Fill it with rubble or gravel, top with inverted turves and cover with a layer of soil.

LAYING LAND DRAINS

1 Dig the trench for the drains at least 30cm (1ft) deep and with a slight fall. Place a layer of coarse grit or fine gravel along the bottom.

2 Traditional clay drains are still used, but you may find plastic equivalents like these at your local builder's merchant. Both kinds are satisfactory. Lay the drains on the bed of gravel.

SOIL CONDITIONERS

1 Dig in plenty of garden compost, well-rotted manure, or any organic matter that will quickly rot down in the soil. Peat and sharp sand will not rot down, but they help to improve the structure of the soil and aid drainage (sharp sand) or moisture-retention (peat or peat substitute).

2 If you can't easily dig more material into the soil because the area has already been planted, use plenty of organic mulches, such as garden compost or chipped bark, which will eventually be worked into the soil.

3 A heavy clay soil can be improved by applying lime (but only if this does not make it too alkaline for the plants you want to grow) and digging in a generous amount of *coarse* sand or grit. Also add plenty of compost or well-rotted manure. Concentrate on improving just a small area, rather than spreading the materials too thinly over a large area.

3 For side drains, use a T-shaped connector designed for the job. To ensure a close fit when using clay drains, score and cut the side drain with a cold chisel. Strike with firm blows to ensure a clean cut.

4 Pack coarse grit or fine gravel around the drains to improve drainage further and to reduce the chance of the pipes becoming clogged.

MAKING GARDEN COMPOST

It's almost impossible to have too much garden compost, so make as much as you can. You can form a compost heap without a container, but if you want to keep your compost looking tidy it's best to buy a bin or compost maker, or build one from scrap wood.

CONSTRUCTING A WOODEN BIN

1 The simplest way to build a wooden compost bin is to buy a kit. The wood will be pre-cut and ready to assemble. Most kits are assembled by slotting the pieces of wood together, or nailing the slats to the corner pieces provided.

2 The kit shown here is quick and easy to make. The pieces are hammered into the slots to form a sturdy bin. Once it has filled with compost, simply lift the entire bin away and start a new compost heap.

READY-MADE COMPOST BINS

A proprietary compost bin with lid.

This bin is suitable for compost or leaves.

MAKING COMPOST

1 To provide good aeration, place twiggy material at the bottom of the heap, then pile on kitchen and garden refuse that will rot down easily. Do not put on thick prunings unless they have been finely shredded first.

2 After adding 15cm (6in) of kitchen or garden refuse, add a layer of manure if possible. This will help to speed up the rotting process.

3 If manure is not available, sprinkle a thin layer of soil over every 15cm (6in) of refuse, to introduce more bacteria into the heap.

4 A proprietary compost activator will help to speed up the rotting process by stimulating the bacterial growth. You should not need to use an activator if the heap has had manure added to it.

TIPS FOR QUICK COMPOST

▊ Use a bin or heap as large as possible – this generates more heat and increases the chance of the material rotting down more quickly.

▊ Keep the material moist – be prepared to water it in dry weather if necessary.

▊ Cover the top in wet weather if necessary to prevent waterlogging.

▊ If possible, let in plenty of air at the base or sides.

▊ In winter, cover the whole heap with an old carpet or something similar, to keep it warm and prevent waterlogging. Compost can take a long time to mature in cold weather.

▊ To speed up the rotting process, fork out the compost after a few weeks, then fork it back into the bin, putting the old material from the outside towards the middle.

FERTILIZERS AND MANURES 1

Most gardeners happily use a combination of organic and inorganic fertilizers, but some prefer the organic-only approach. The important point to remember is that feeding will make a difference, especially to vegetables, seedlings and plants grown in containers. The benefit to shrubs and trees is usually less obvious, and it is best only to feed these in response to a known deficiency.

APPLYING FERTILIZERS

1 Apply fertilizers as evenly as possible. Divide unplanted ground into strips 90cm (3ft) wide, and work along these in 90cm (3ft) 'bites', scattering the appropriate amount of fertilizer for the area. Alternatively use a wheeled fertilizer spreader.

2 Rake it in when the area is complete. This will help to distribute the fertilizer more evenly as well as work it into the soil.

3 Vegetables sometimes need a boost during growth. Scatter the fertilizer along either side of the row, keeping it off the leaves. Hoe it in afterwards.

4 Scatter the fertilizer in a circle around established shrubs and other large plants. This will concentrate it where the active feeding roots are, with less chance of feeding weeds. Do not apply the fertilizer beyond the spread of the plant, and keep it away from the stem.

5 Hoe the fertilizer in, so that it penetrates more rapidly. Unless rain is forecast soon, water it in thoroughly so that it is available to the plants more quickly.

INORGANIC FERTILIZERS

Ammonium sulphate (sulphate of ammonia) supplies nitrogen, but makes the soil more acid.

Nitro-chalk supplies nitrogen without making the soil more acid.

Potassium sulphate (sulphate of potash) supplies potassium.

Superphosphate of lime (sometimes shortened to 'superphosphate') supplies phosphorus. Triple superphosphate is similar but almost three times stronger, so make sure that you apply the right kind of superphosphate of lime at an appropriate rate.

Balanced fertilizers (such as Growmore in the UK – which is a formulation, not a trade name) contain all the main nutrients: nitrogen, phosphorus and potassium.

Compound fertilizers are usually the same as balanced fertilizers, but do not always contain all three major nutrients.

Controlled- and slow-release fertilizers contain the major nutrients in a form that is released slowly over a period of months. In the case of controlled-release fertilizers, this is regulated by the temperature of the soil.

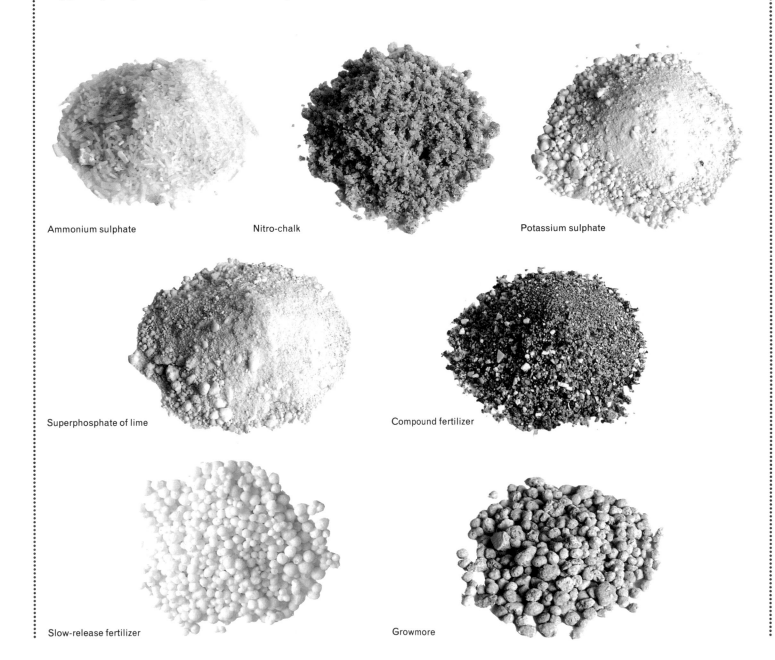

Ammonium sulphate

Nitro-chalk

Potassium sulphate

Superphosphate of lime

Compound fertilizer

Slow-release fertilizer

Growmore

FERTILIZERS AND MANURES 2

Organic gardeners prefer to use fertilizers that occur as natural products. Most of them are useful even if you do not garden organically.

ORGANIC FERTILIZERS

Blood, fish and bonemeal contains all the major nutrients. The nitrogen content is released quickly.

Bonemeal is a popular slow-acting fertilizer containing mainly phosphorus but also some nitrogen. 'Steamed' bonemeal should be safe to handle – unsterilized bonemeal carries a very small risk of harbouring diseases.

Dried animal manures are available in various types. They usually contain only a trace of the major nutrients, but a full range of trace elements (those nutrients needed only in very small quantities).

Dried blood is a fast-acting nitrogenous fertilizer. Use it when the plants need a quick boost of growth during the summer.

Fish meal contains nitrogen and phosphorus.

Hoof and horn contains nitrogen in a form that is released slowly. It is a more suitable source of nitrogen than dried blood for sustained growth.

Liquid animal manures contain a small amount of all the major nutrients, plus a full range of trace elements.

Liquid seaweed contains a useful amount of nitrogen and potassium, but only a trace of phosphorus. It is good for supplying trace elements and some growth hormones.

Seaweed meal contains all the major nutrients, plus many minor ones and trace elements. It is a very good all-round fertilizer, but is best applied when the soil is warm so that the bacteria can break it down.

Wood ash – the exact chemical analysis will depend on the material burned, but there will be a useful amount of potassium and a small amount of phosphorus.

BULKY MANURES AND COMPOST

Garden compost, well-rotted animal manures, and bulky organic materials such as spent mushroom compost and spent hops usually add only small amounts of fertilizer. They are invaluable, however, because they help to improve the soil structure, its water-holding capacity, and even the ability of the soil to retain nutrients applied from other sources.

Dried chicken manure

Blood, fish and bonemeal

Bonemeal

Dried blood

1 Green manuring is a way of adding humus to the soil without making a compost heap. First fork over the ground cleared of an earlier crop.

2 Scatter mustard seed (or any other type of seed sold for green manuring) so that it covers the ground quite thickly.

3 Rake over the soil to bury the mustard seed completely.

4 When the mustard is about 30cm (12in) high, and before it flowers and sets seed, dig it into the ground. It will eventually rot and release both humus and nutrients for a later crop.

Liquid seaweed

Fish meal

Seaweed meal

Hoof and horn

WATERING

Watering by hand is a chore that most gardeners prefer to avoid, but there are ways to make the job easier, and automatic watering systems will eliminate the hard work and be better for the plants.

DRIP FEEDS

1 A system like this one will solve most of your watering problems. You can run both spray and drip nozzles off the same system. Connect the master unit to a hose from the mains. The master unit reduces the water pressure and contains a filter that can be removed for cleaning.

2 Run the main supply tube where it will not be too visible, such as beneath a hedge, or submerged just beneath the soil.

3 Connect the smaller-diameter branch tubes with the special connectors wherever you need to take water to a particular part of the garden.

4 Use drip-feed heads to water containers and individual plants in a border. The special pegs provided will enable you to hold the tube in a suitable position.

5 Use a spray head for more general watering, such as for flower beds or rows of vegetables. This particular system offers a range of nozzles to provide different water droplet sizes and areas covered.

GARDENING BASICS

CHOOSING AN APPROPRIATE SPRINKLER

Oscillating sprinklers are useful for rectangular lawns and seed beds. They can usually be adjusted to cover areas of different sizes.

Static sprinklers are intended mainly for lawns, but they generally water in a circular pattern, so you will have to keep moving them around to achieve even coverage. They are mostly inexpensive.

Rotating sprinklers water in a circular pattern. The droplets are thrown out by rotating arms driven by the water pressure. They usually cover a wider area than static sprinklers.

If you want to water a flower bed or vegetable plot, buy a version with a head on a long spike. The head must be clear of surrounding foliage.

Pulse-jet sprinklers have a single jet on a central pivot that rotates in a series of pulses, each time ejecting a spurt of water. These water in a circular pattern, but are efficient and can cover a very wide area. Those intended for lawns usually have a low base, but if the water needs to be thrown clear of surrounding foliage, buy one on a long stem.

Oscillating sprinkler

Static sprinkler

Rotating sprinkler

Pulse-jet sprinkler

TAPS AND TIMERS

An outdoor tap is invaluable, and essential if you have a drip-feed watering system. Outdoor tap kits are readily available, and these contain all the parts and instructions for fitting.

In the UK you must fit a non-return valve. These are widely

available, and some outdoor taps already have them fitted.

If you have installed an automatic watering system, go one step further and install a tap computer that will turn the water supply on and off at programmed times, even when you are not there.

SEEP HOSES

Seep hoses are designed to be laid along the ground for long-term watering. The tiny perforations deliver the water slowly so that it seeps well down into the soil. You can use seep hoses in flower beds or borders, but they are especially useful for irrigating rows of fruit or vegetables.

SEEPAGE HOSE

Some seepage hoses are made of a porous rubber. The water seeps slowly from the surface. Lay a seepage hose on top of the soil like an ordinary seep hose, or bury it in a shallow slit trench 10–15cm (4–6in) deep. You may find this visually more acceptable in a shrub or herbaceous border.

Weeding Beds And Borders

Weeds not only look unsightly but they also affect the growth of your plants by competing for water and nutrients. To win the battle against weeds, you need a plan of campaign and to carry it through with determination. Once you are in control, weeding should be no more than a minor occasional chore.

HAND-WEEDING

1 Some hand-weeding will always be necessary, but forking out deep-rooted perennials such as nettles and dandelions should be required only when you clear the ground. Later, seedlings should never be allowed to become so well established. Use a fork to loosen the roots, and hold the main stem close to the soil so that you can pull up the whole root system. If the root won't lift without tearing, dig deeper.

2 Even difficult perennial weeds are easy to control if you remove them while they are still young. Make sure that you remove the whole root, but a hand fork should be adequate for lifting the plant.

3 Regular hoeing will keep most weeds under control. Hoe in dry weather, and slice the weeds off below the surface, holding the hoe so that the blade is parallel to the soil's surface. This is a Dutch hoe, useful for weeding along straight rows, but there are other designs and proprietary hoes that you might find more useful for specific situations.

4 A hand cultivator with prongs which may be removed can be useful for loosening the soil and weeds along rows of vegetables. However, it is not as efficient as a hoe when slicing off weeds.

GARDENING BASICS

CHEMICAL WEEDING

1 Use a chemical weedkiller if you want to clear the ground of weeds quickly. Some weedkillers will just kill the top growth, so are best for annual weeds, while others will kill the roots too. Others will inhibit the growth of new seedlings. Be sure to choose one appropriate to your needs.

Spray drift from a weedkiller is a real hazard to your plants. Always choose a calm day for spraying and fit a dribble bar to the watering can. Hold the bar close to the ground. Keep a watering can exclusively for applying weedkillers and label it clearly.

2 Most weedkillers will begin to act within days, and after a week the weeds will show clear signs of dying. Some weedkillers are inactivated by contact with the soil, and you can sow or plant as soon as you have cleared away the dead growth. If you use a weedkiller that is translocated to the roots to kill difficult perennial weeds, wait until the top growth has died down before removing the weeds – this gives the weedkiller time to work properly.

3 If you have difficult, deep-rooted perennial weeds growing among desirable plants, making spraying impossible, paint a translocated weedkiller (such as one based on glyphosate) on to individual weeds.

MULCH CONTROL

2 Where appearance matters, such as in a flower or shrub border, cover any bare ground with a 5cm (2in) layer of chipped bark or other decorative mulch.

1 Black polythene sheeting controls weeds very effectively. Where appearance does not matter, lay it along the rows. Tuck the edges in a shallow trench and cover with soil, or just weight down with bricks. Alternatively, hold in place with proprietary pegs sold for the purpose.

WEEDING LAWNS AND PATHS

When hand-weeding was the only option, a weed-free lawn or path was either a dream or exceptionally hard work. Nowadays selective weedkillers, which attack most of the weeds but not the grass, enable anyone to achieve a super lawn . . . and long-lasting path weedkillers mean clear paths all year round with just one or two applications.

LAWN WEEDKILLERS

1 Most selective lawn weed-killers are diluted and applied as a liquid. To be sure of covering the area evenly, use two lengths of string to mark out the width of the dribble bar used with your watering can.

2 At the end of each row, move one of the strings across to mark out the next strip. Always follow the manufacturer's suggested rate of application.

3 If your lawn also needs feeding, save time with a weed-and-feed for lawns. This contains a combined fertilizer and weedkiller, but use it only when the lawn needs weeding, and follow the manufacturer's advice. There are different mixtures for spring, summer and autumn use. Apply with a fertilizer spreader if you want to save even more time.

4 It is wasteful to apply a selective weedkiller to the whole lawn if you have just a few weeds in small patches. You can apply a liquid weedkiller to small patches of lawn, but a wipe-on stick containing a selective weedkiller is a quick, cheap and easy method of dealing with just a few isolated weeds.

HAND-WEEDING A LAWN

1 Weeding trowels are useful for prising up weeds such as dandelions and daisies. Push the tool in just behind the root and lift the plant with a lever action as you pull with the other hand. Even deep-rooted plants can usually be removed like this.

2 Firm the soil again afterwards to make it less suitable for weed seedlings to germinate. If you have had to lift a lot of weeds that were close together, there may be a bare patch. It is worth sprinkling a few grass seeds over the patch rather than leaving bare soil for more weed seedlings to grow.

DEALING WITH COARSE GRASS

If you have a small clump of very coarse grass growing in your lawn, either dig it up and reseed the area, or keep slashing through it with a knife. This will eventually weaken it and allow the finer grasses to grow over the area.

PATH WEEDKILLERS

1 Path weedkillers will kill all plants that they touch, and most will remain active in the soil for many months. Always choose a still day to reduce the risk of wind blowing the spray around the garden. A watering can with a dribble bar will apply larger drops than most sprayers and these are less likely to blow around.

2 Shield plants with a sheet of cardboard, plywood or plastic if you are applying a weedkiller to a path near a border.

PEST CONTROL 1:
APHIDS AND OTHER SAP-SUCKERS

Sap-sucking insects are particularly unpleasant pests because they transmit virus diseases by injecting infected sap from one plant into another. They also cause distorted growth if they attack developing buds, and generally weaken the plants that they feed on. Always deal with aphids promptly.

IDENTIFICATION

Aphids are among the best-known insect pests. Greenfly and blackfly are the common ones, but there are many species, some affecting the roots of plants rather than the

CHEMICAL CONTROL

Many leaf-sucking insects hide on the undersides of leaves. Always make sure that you cover the undersides of the leaves as well as the tops – especially if using a contact insecticide.

leaves. Foliage may be sticky from the honeydew excreted by the aphids – with a black mould.
Control with any contact insecticide recommended for aphids. Systemic insecticide is likely to be more effective on ornamental plants.
Green controls include insecticidal soaps and pirimicarb.
Leaf hoppers are usually green or yellow insects 2–3mm ($\frac{1}{16}$–$\frac{1}{8}$in) long. They leap when disturbed.
Control with most contact and systemic insecticides.
Red spider mites are tiny creatures about 2mm ($\frac{1}{16}$in) long. You are more likely to notice their fine, silky webs and a pale mottling on the upper surface of leaves rather than the pests themselves.
Control with a contact insecticide, or a systemic insecticide.
Green control is best achieved with the predatory mite *Phytoseiulus persimilis* and high humidity.
Scale insects are immobile and scale-like in appearance, usually yellow, brown, dark grey or white, and up to 6mm ($\frac{1}{4}$in) long.
Control with a contact insecticide recommended for scale.

Thrips are narrow brownish-black insects up to 2mm ($\frac{1}{16}$in) long. Affected leaves have a silvery-white discoloration on the upper surface.
Control with a systemic insecticide.
Green control is best with a 'natural' relatively harmless insecticide such as one based on pyrethrum. Be prepared to spray frequently.
Whitefly look like tiny white moths, and often rise up in a cloud when disturbed. The wingless nymphs are whitish-green and scale-like.
Control with any of the contact insecticides recommended for whitefly, but be prepared to repeat the treatment frequently.
Green control is with a parasitic wasp, *Encarsia formosa*, but this is suitable only for the greenhouse.

BIOLOGICAL CONTROL

Biological controls are available for some sap-sucking pests. *Encarsia formosa* is a parasitic wasp that will help to control whitefly. Hang the pack on the plants that you want to protect. The parasites will emerge and in time will start to breed.

Blackfly   Whitefly   Symptoms of red spider mite   Leaf hopper damage   Scale

PEST CONTROL 2:
LEAF-EATERS

Leaf-eating pests can soon devastate a plant. If the culprits are caterpillars you will easily identify the cause, but many leaf-eaters move on, so tracking them down may call for a little deduction.

IDENTIFICATION

Caterpillars come in many shapes and sizes, but you will certainly recognize them even if you don't

CHEMICAL CONTROL

Slug pellets are very effective at controlling slugs and snails. Most are coloured blue to make them unattractive to birds. If you are worried about pets eating the pellets, place them in pieces of narrow drainpipe or something similar.

It is unnecessary to space them more closely than is recommended by the manufacturer – about 15cm (6in) apart is close enough.

know the species. You will find them on the affected leaves.
Control with derris dust or another contact insecticide recommended for caterpillars.
Green controls include picking off by hand and spraying with the bacterial control *Bacillus thuringiensis*.

Earwigs are yellowish-brown insects about 12mm (½in) long, with curved pincers at the rear.
Control with insecticidal powders for crawling insects, dusted around the base of the plant, or sprayed on at dusk, which are more effective than normal contact sprays.
Green control is to make a trap of a pot stuffed with straw, placed on top of a cane. The earwigs will shelter in this during the day. Empty the pot periodically and destroy the insects.

Slugs and snails are too well-known to need description. Symptoms range from holes in the leaves to foliage that is completely eaten, or stripped down to the main stalks. The pest may have moved on or gone into hiding, but slime trails are often a give-away.

Control with slug pellets.
Green control involves making or buying beer traps so that the pests drown in a state of intoxication. Protect vulnerable plants in the spring by sprinkling coarse grit around crowns and new shoots.

Weevils eat irregularly-shaped holes around the edges of leaves. The mature insects are usually grey or black with a short snout and elbowed antennae.
Control by spraying with an insecticide recommended for the pest, preferably at dusk.
Green control by biological control is being developed.

BIOLOGICAL CONTROL

Many kinds of caterpillar can be controlled with a bacterium that causes a disease in the insects. If you spray the food plants of the pest species (such as cabbages) you should not upset the health of the population of decorative butterflies that feed on weeds.

Mix up the spray as recommended by the manufacturer, and spray before the caterpillars have become a major problem.

Caterpillar damage

Snail damage

Earwig damage

Slug damage

Weevils

PEST CONTROL 3: ROOT-EATERS

Root pests often go unnoticed until the plants collapse, but many of them can be controlled successfully if you are vigilant.

IDENTIFICATION

Cutworms and leatherjackets
Cutworms are the caterpillars of various moths, and have a typical caterpillar shape. They are usually brown and live in the soil, though they may feed above soil level at night. The base of the stem is usually gnawed, and the plant slowly wilts and will probably die. Leatherjackets are the larvae of daddy-long-legs, or crane flies, and have tubular grey bodies about 2.5–4cm (1–1½in) long.
Control by treating the affected plants with a soil insecticide as soon as you notice the damage.
Green control consists of winter digging where applicable, to expose the grubs to birds, and picking the pests off by hand whenever you find them.

Root flies are numerous, and affect vegetables such as carrots and onions, but also bulbs. There are many different species, and it is the larvae that do the damage by eating the roots.
Control is difficult or impossible once the grubs are in the roots. Where these pests are known to be a problem, use a soil insecticide when planting or sowing.
Green control consists of always firming the soil around the roots when planting or thinning, and not leaving thinnings on the surface (the smell may attract the flies). Carrot fly can be deterred by erecting a polythene barrier about 45cm (18in) tall around the plants. This works because the pests only fly close to the ground.

BIOLOGICAL CONTROL

Carrot flies keep close to the ground, so a low physical barrier like a fine net mesh may be enough to prevent them laying their eggs around the plants.

Weevils There are several species, and it is the grubs that damage plant roots. If a small plant collapses and you find small curved white grubs with brown heads and no legs on the remains of the roots, these are likely to be weevil grubs.
Control is difficult, and soil insecticides have only a limited degree of success.
Green control is possible with a nematode, which affects the grubs, but this solution is only just becoming widely available at the time of writing.

CHEMICAL CONTROL

Ordinary insecticides are not very effective in the soil. Use a product recommended for soil pests. Some are available as powders to sprinkle on affected areas, others are sprays to be applied to the soil.

Root fly larvae

Root fly damage

Grubs of weevils

DISEASE CONTROL 1: LEAF DISEASES

Fungus diseases affect the leaves of many plants, and often they are difficult to control. Where possible grow varieties that have a disease resistance, and always spray or remove affected leaves at the first sign of trouble.

IDENTIFICATION

Downy mildew looks like a fluffy or mealy white growth on the surface of the leaf. This may be most obvious on the underside, with just brown or yellow blotches on the top surface.

Control by removing the affected leaves, then spraying the plant with a fungicide recommended for this disease. Sprays that control powdery mildew may not be very effective against downy mildew.

Green control consists of picking off affected leaves as soon as the disease is noticed. Make sure that the plants have good ventilation and are not overcrowded.

Leaf spots affect many plants, and rose black spot is just one kind. The spots or blotches are usually black, brown or yellow.

Control is best achieved by a systemic fungicide (except for edible crops).

Green control is difficult, but good garden hygiene (destroying affected leaves promptly) will limit the spread of these diseases.

Powdery mildew looks like a white powdery deposit on the leaves, and is most commonly found on the upper surface.

Downy mildew

Leaf spot

Powdery mildew

Rust

Control and green control are as for downy mildew, except that you have a wider choice of chemicals.

Rusts vary in appearance depending on the type, but most cause yellowish patches on the upper surface of the leaves and corresponding small brown or

BIOLOGICAL CONTROL

You can achieve a lot simply by picking off diseased leaves as soon as they are noticed, to prevent the problem spreading. Always collect dead leaves at the end of the season, but do not use diseased leaves for compost.

orange patches on the reverse sides of the leaves.

Control with one of the few fungicides that control rust reasonably well (check the label to see if the product is recommended for rust – many fungicides are not effective). Remove affected leaves to prevent the disease spreading.

Green control is best achieved by picking off and destroying all affected leaves as soon as they are noticed, and ensuring adequate spacing and ventilation.

CHEMICAL CONTROL

Roses and other plants prone to fungus diseases are best sprayed on a regular basis with a systemic fungicide to keep them healthy and disease-free.

DISEASE CONTROL 2: ROOT DISEASES

Most root diseases are a minor inconvenience that crops up from time to time, but club-root is a serious problem that will restrict the types of plants that you can grow successfully.

IDENTIFICATION

Blackleg affects cuttings. The base turns black, shrinks and becomes soft. The cutting eventually dies.
Control is impossible once blackleg occurs, but using a rooting hormone that contains a fungicide may prevent it happening.
Green control is not practical – just remove and destroy affected cuttings promptly.
Club-root affects members of the *Cruciferae* family, especially brassicas such as cabbages and swedes and a few ornamentals such as wallflowers. The roots become swollen and distorted, and growth is very stunted.
Control of club-root is difficult because the disease remains in the soil for many years. Use a proprietary club-root dip before planting out the seedlings.
Green control is best achieved by growing the seedlings in pots of sterilized compost – they will get off to a good start and be better able to resist the worst effects of the disease. Keep down weeds that are a potential source of infection.
Foot and root rots affect a number of plants such as peas, beans, tomatoes, cucumbers and even bedding plants such as petunias. The roots turn black and the base of the stem starts to rot.
Control with chemicals is not practical for foot and root rots.
Green control is the most effective: try to avoid growing the same plants in the same ground each year, raise plants in sterilized compost and destroy affected plants as soon as they are noticed.
Storage rots affect bulbs and corms in storage, as well as stored onions. Soft patches appear, and sometimes the surface area is covered with fungal growth.
Control by dusting non-edible bulbs, tubers and corms with a fungicide before storing.
Green control is effective. Always make sure that the bulbs are dry before storing them, and keep in a cool but frost-free, airy place. Check every few weeks and remove any soft bulbs before they can affect the others.

CHEMICAL CONTROL

Non-edible bulbs, corms and tubers will be less likely to rot in store if you first treat them with a fungicide. Dust them with a suitable powder, or use a fungicidal dip (be sure to dry them off thoroughly afterwards).

BIOLOGICAL CONTROL

Bulbs, corms and tubers will be less likely to rot if you hang them up in something where air can circulate freely, like a net or even a pair of old tights or stockings.

Blackleg

PHYSIOLOGICAL AND OTHER PROBLEMS

Some problems that at first appear to be caused by pests or diseases have physiological causes (like wind chill or sun scorch). Others are caused by accidents with weedkillers, or even by nutritional deficiencies in the soil.

IDENTIFICATION

Cold damage is most likely to occur on evergreens that are not completely hardy. The leaves are blackened or brown, and often puckered or withered. Prune out affected parts – many plants will soon outgrow limited damage.

Fasciated stems can be caused by many factors, such as injury or a genetic quirk. The stems are flattened and may look as though two stems are fused together. No harm is caused to the plant.

Iron and manganese deficiencies are most likely on chalky soils. Both create similar symptoms: yellowing leaves, especially at the edges or between the veins. If caused by a soil with a high pH, apply sequestered iron or trace elements in a chelated or fritted formulation.

Nitrogen deficiency shows itself in pale green leaves, sometimes mottled or flushed yellow. Growth is usually slow. Feed with a high-nitrogen fertilizer.

Potassium deficiency shows itself in leaves that look prematurely autumnal, with a yellow or purplish flush or blotches, and brown margins. The leaves sometimes roll inwards. Apply a sulphate of potash or some other fertilizer high in potassium.

Sun scorch happens behind unshaded glass in a greenhouse or where the temperature is exceptionally high. Brown patches on the upper exposed surface of the leaf are early signs, but the edges of the leaves may also turn brown and brittle. Solve the problem by providing better shading for the plant during hot, sunny weather and plenty of ventilation.

Weedkiller damage depends on the type of weedkiller involved. Selective hormone weedkillers used in lawns will cause distorted growth if they drift on to nearby ornamental plants. Contact weedkillers usually cause pale or bleached areas on the foliage, which may turn almost white. Eventually it turns brown and black. There is nothing you can do, except to be more careful when applying another time.

Viruses come in many forms, causing different symptoms. Usually the leaves have a mottled pattern, or a yellowish mosaic effect, or yellow stripes, and the plant is generally stunted. Not all viruses are regarded as undesirable – some striped flowers and variegated leaves which are caused by virus infections are regarded as attractive. Generally, however, all plants that have been affected by a virus should be pulled up and destroyed as soon as possible.

Cold damage

Manganese deficiency

Iron deficiency

Fasciated stem

Nitrogen deficiency

Sun scorch

Virus infection

SOWING IN POTS AND TRAYS

Tender bedding plants must be started off indoors or in the greenhouse. Sow in trays if you need a lot of plants, but if you need just a few, sow in pots to save space. Many hardy plants such as rock plants and hardy border perennials can be sown in pots and trays, but to save space indoors you can put them out in a cold frame to germinate.

GARDENING BASICS

SOWING IN POTS

1 For border perennials, rock plants, house plants and shrubs, where you will not need many plants, sow in pots to save space. Make yourself a rounded presser to firm down the compost, or improvise with a jam-jar or something similar.

2 Sprinkle the seeds over the compost as evenly as possible, using the sand technique described below if the seed is very fine. Stand the pot in a bowl of water and let it seep through to moisten the compost. Remove it and let it drain.

3 Insert a label then cover with a sheet of glass or put the pot into a propagator if the seeds need warmth for germination.

4 Some seeds, particularly alpines and shrubs, do not need much warmth and are often better in cool conditions initially. Place these in a cold frame instead of a propagator. Plunging the pots in sand reduces the risk of the compost drying out.

SOWING FINE SEED

1 If the seed is very fine and difficult to handle, mix it with a small quantity of silver sand to make even distribution easier.

2 Sprinkle the sand and seed mix as evenly as possible between your finger and thumb, as if sprinkling salt over food. Very fine seed will need only a very shallow covering or no covering at all.

1 Fill the tray loosely with a sterilized compost suitable for seeds (do not use a potting compost). Strike off the compost so it is level with the rim, then press it down with a piece of wood that will fit inside the tray. Leave the compost about 12mm (½in) below the rim. Water the tray with a fine-rosed can *before* sowing. If you water afterwards you might wash the seeds away or cause them to drift to one side of the tray.

2 Sprinkle the seeds as thinly as possible over the surface. Large seeds can be spaced individually. To space medium-sized seeds fold over a piece of stiff paper to hold the seeds, then tap it with a finger as you move it over the surface.

3 Cover the seeds by sifting more compost over the top. Always check the seed packet to find whether or not the seeds should be covered. Some seeds germinate better if exposed to light.

4 Cover the tray with a sheet of glass to prevent the compost drying out. If you don't have a sheet of glass, place the tray in a polythene bag. Tuck the end under or seal it with a plastic-covered wire twist-tie. Don't forget to label the tray.

5 Turn the glass over, or the bag inside out, daily to prevent condensation drips becoming a problem.

6 You should remove the glass or plastic bag as soon as the seeds begin to germinate. If you leave them covered for too long, the humid environment created may encourage the growth of fungal diseases that can kill the seedlings.

PRICKING OUT

As soon as seedlings are large enough to handle, prick them out into pots or trays of potting compost so they have the space and nutrients necessary for healthy growth.

PRICKING OUT INTO TRAYS

1 Fill the tray with a sterilized potting compost. Strike it level and firm to leave the compost about 12mm (½in) below the rim.

2 Use a small dibber or a tool designed for pricking out seedlings to loosen the compost and lift out each seedling with as much compost as possible attached.

3 Use the small dibber or planting tool to make a hole deep enough to take the roots, and transplant the seedling while holding it by one of its seed leaves (the first leaves to open). Firm the compost gently around the roots. Space the seedlings about 2.5–5cm (1–2in) apart, depending on the needs of the plant.

4 Water the plants thoroughly after transplanting, using a watering can with a fine rose. Shade from direct sunlight for a couple of days.

PRICKING OUT INTO MODULES

Pricking out into modules, or trays with pre-formed compartments, will ensure even spacing and cause less root damage when you transplant the seedlings.

TRANSPLANTING INTO POTS

1 Pot plants such as cyclamen, greenhouse plants like tomatoes and cucumbers, and large bedding plants such as dahlias are best pricked out into individual pots instead of trays. The seedlings have more space to grow and more compost to sustain them. Loosen the plants as described for pricking out into trays, but place them in small 8–10cm (3–4in) pots.

2 After watering, keep the pots out of direct sunlight for a couple of days. Square pots are more space-saving than round pots for the same volume of compost.

PLUGS AND POT-READY PLANTS

1 Seedlings are sometimes sold in 'plugs' (small individual blocks of compost). You can also grow your own seedlings like this, using the small plastic trays designed for the purpose (sow one or two seeds in each cell, and thin to one plant if necessary).

2 Transplant the seedlings into seed trays or pots, spacing them as you would seedlings sown in a tray. Young plants are sometimes sold by nurseries and garden centres in larger plugs of compost, or in special small peat containers. These larger plants are best potted up individually rather than grown in trays.

Sowing in 'cells' or modules saves the tricky and time-consuming job of pricking out. Just sow a couple of seeds in each cell then pull out any surplus if more than one germinates. The technique is suitable for most bedding plants and many vegetables that are started off in the greenhouse.

BORECOLE DWARF GREEN CURLED H

SOWING HARDY ANNUALS

Hardy annuals are undemanding plants that you can sow directly into the garden, where the plants are to flower. Provided you thin them out and water in dry weather while they are small, you will have masses of colourful flowers for the minimum of effort.

SOWING IN ROWS

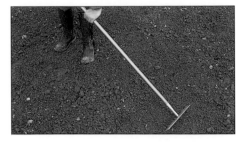

1 Make sure that the area is free of weeds, then rake the ground level. Break down any large lumps of earth so that the seeds have fine soil in which to germinate.

2 For a bright bed of annuals, mark out the areas in which each kind is to grow, using sand or grit to indicate the boundary of each drift of colour.

3 Take out shallow drills with a hoe or the corner of a rake, at a spacing appropriate to the type of plant. Alternate the direction of the drills in each marked area, as this will make the bed look less strictly regimented.

4 Sow the seeds as evenly as possible. Space large or pelleted seeds individually, otherwise take a few seeds at a time and scatter them as evenly as possible along the drill.

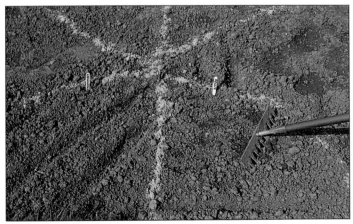

5 Label each section, then rake the soil level to cover the seeds.

6 Water whenever the weather is dry until all the seedlings have germinated and are well established.

Hardy annuals are the easiest of all flowers to grow. They can be sown where they are to flower, usually bloom quickly, and in the majority of cases are bright and cheerful. These are godetias.

SOWING BROADCAST

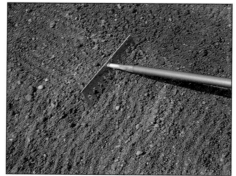

1 Packets of mixed annuals and groups of one type that are to be grown in a less formal way can be sown broadcast (scattered randomly). At the seedling stage, however, it is more difficult to tell which are annuals and which are weed seedlings, but this is a quicker way to sow. Just scatter the seeds over the area as evenly as possible.

2 Rake the seeds in to distribute and bury them. Rake first in one direction and then at right angles.

THINNING

Thin the seedlings while still young to prevent overcrowding. Hold the soil down on either side of the plant you want to retain while pulling out the unwanted plants. Leave the seedlings spaced at the distances recommended on the packet. Water after thinning if the weather is dry.

SOWING ALPINES AND SHRUBS

Alpine and tree and shrub seeds often need to undergo a period of cold weather, and many germinate better if you sow them in the autumn and overwinter them in a cold frame.

1 Fill a small pot with a loam-based seed compost and firm it gently to provide a flat surface for sowing.

2 Sow the seed fairly thickly as germination is often poor or erratic, but do not let the seeds touch one another.

3 Cover the seeds with more potting compost, then sprinkle grit or coarse sand over the surface to discourage the growth of algae and keep the surface well aerated.

4 Plunge the pots up to their rims in a cold frame to keep the compost moist. If the seeds are fleshy and attractive to mice, cover the pots with a sheet of glass.

PRICKING OUT

Don't forget to label the pots — especially if you have sown more than one kind of seed. And remember to keep the compost watered whenever necessary. Seedlings will usually start to germinate in the spring and during the summer. Prick them out and grow on in pots or in rows in a nursery bed (see opposite).

LEFT Aubretias are particularly easy alpines to raise from seed, and they flower quickly. Although they generally do not grow true to type from seed, they are often just as good as named varieties from cuttings.

BIENNIALS AND PERENNIALS

1 An easy way to grow biennials and border perennials is to sow the seeds in a seed bed in the garden in late spring or early summer. Choose a vacant piece of ground for sowing, making sure that it is neither too dry nor too shaded.

2 Take out shallow drills in rows about 23cm (9in) apart, and sow the seeds thinly. Water the rows gently, then rake the soil over the seeds.

3 If you have sown too thickly, thin some of the seedlings. When the seedlings are 5–8cm (2–3in) high, prepare another piece of ground where the plants can grow on until the autumn. Rake in a general garden fertilizer.

4 Space the seedlings 15–23cm (6–9in) apart to allow them enough space to grow during the summer. Water well.

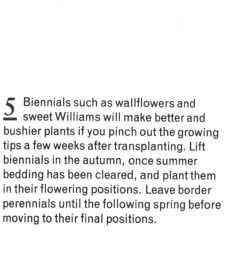

5 Biennials such as wallflowers and sweet Williams will make better and bushier plants if you pinch out the growing tips a few weeks after transplanting. Lift biennials in the autumn, once summer bedding has been cleared, and plant them in their flowering positions. Leave border perennials until the following spring before moving to their final positions.

SOFTWOOD AND GREENWOOD CUTTINGS

Softwood and greenwood cuttings root quickly and easily, and you can take them from popular plants like pelargoniums (geraniums) and fuchsias. Greenwood cuttings are similar to softwood cuttings, but are taken from the soft tip of the stem after the first flush of early growth has slowed down.

KEEPING CUTTINGS FRESH

Softwood cuttings soon wilt, so put them in a polythene bag until you are ready to insert them into the compost.

TAKING SOFTWOOD CUTTINGS

1 Many shrubs, as well as pelargoniums (geraniums), can be propagated from the soft new shoots produced during the early flush of growth. The length of the cutting is not critical, but do cut below the third leaf or pair of leaves from the tip.

2 Trim off the lowest pair of leaves. If the plant has stipules (small scale-like growths at the base of each leaf stalk), as pelargoniums do, pull these off too. Trim the base of the stem with a sharp knife or blade, cutting straight across the stem just below a leaf joint.

3 Dip the cut tip of each cutting into a rooting powder containing a fungicide.

4 Use a dibber to make a hole in a pot of cuttings compost for the cutting.

5 Insert the cuttings around the edge of the pot, without overcrowding them. Alternatively, place each cutting in a small individual pot. After watering, place in a warm and humid propagator, or cover with a polythene bag, and keep in a warm light place out of direct sunlight. If a number of cuttings have been planted together in one pot, pot up individually once each plant has formed plenty of roots.

TAKING GREENWOOD CUTTINGS

1 Take the cuttings once the new growth has begun to slow down – usually in early summer. The length will depend on the plant, but for most shrubs remove the top 10cm (4in) of the shoot.

2 Put the cuttings into a polythene bag or a bowl of water until you are ready to prepare them, otherwise they will wilt rapidly.

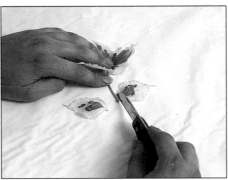

3 Shorten the length of each cutting to about 8cm (3in), though you must adjust this to suit the plant. Cut straight across the stem just below a leaf joint.

4 Trim the leaves from the bottom half of the cutting, using a sharp knife.

5 Dip the cut ends into a rooting hormone, to ensure speedy rooting.

6 Insert the cuttings around the edge of a pot, then water with a fungicide and leave to drain.

7 Place the pot in a warm and humid propagator in a light place out of direct sunlight. If you don't have a propagator, cover the pot with a polythene bag instead.

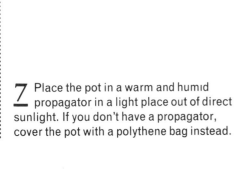

BASAL STEM CUTTINGS

Basal stem cuttings can be taken in spring from many herbaceous plants that produce a cluster of new shoots from the soil level at this time. It's also a good method if you want to propagate more dahlias than division of the tubers would give you.

TAKING DELPHINIUM CUTTINGS

1 Use the basal shoots of delphiniums and lupins to make new plants. Remove the shoots when they are about 8–10cm (3–4in) long, cutting them off just above the surface.

2 Trim the cuttings cleanly with a sharp knife across the end, and remove any low leaves that would be below compost level when the cutting has been inserted. Dip the ends into a rooting hormone.

3 Insert the cuttings, one to a pot or two or three around the edge of a pot, and firm the compost gently. A mixture of peat and sand or a rooting compost should be used. Cover the cuttings to provide a humid atmosphere until they root.

Chrysanthemum

TAKING DAHLIA CUTTINGS

1 In late winter place the tubers in boxes or deep trays and pack moist compost or peat around them. Keep in a warm, light place.

2 When the shoots have grown to about 8cm (3in) long, cut them off close to the tuber.

3 Remove the lowest leaves from each cutting, and trim the cuttings straight just below a leaf joint with a sharp knife or razor blade.

4 Dip the cut ends into a rooting hormone, then insert several cuttings into each pot of rooting compost. Keep moist and pot up individually once they have rooted.

TAKING CHRYSANTHEMUM CUTTINGS

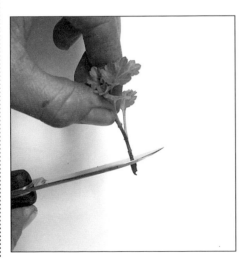

1 Whether the cuttings have been placed in boxes in the greenhouse or the plants have been overwintered outdoors, cut off young shoots about 3–5cm (1¼–2in) long. Pull off the lowest leaves and trim the end with a knife.

2 Insert the cuttings around the edge of a pot. They will usually root without a rooting hormone, but using one will improve the rate and speed of rooting.

3 Cover the pot with a polythene bag, inflated to ensure that it does not touch the cuttings. Check the cuttings regularly, turning the bag to avoid condensation dripping onto the leaves. Remove any leaves that start to rot.

Semi-ripe (also called semi-mature) cuttings are an excellent way to propagate a wide range of shrubs. Mid and late summer are ideal times to take them, and most cuttings will have formed roots within a month or two – some will root after just a couple of weeks.

TAKING SEMI-RIPE CUTTINGS

1 Take cuttings from shoots that are more or less fully grown, except for the tips. The wood at the base should be beginning to harden even though the tip may still be soft. Make the cutting 5–10cm (2–4in) long, depending on the shrub.

2 Strip the lower leaves from each cutting, then trim it to a suitable length if necessary.

3 Use a rooting hormone, dipping just the cut end into the powder or liquid. If using a powder, dip the end of the cutting into water first, so the powder adheres more easily.

4 Semi-ripe cuttings taken during the summer will root in the open ground provided you keep them watered, but they will do better in a garden frame. Make a slit with a trowel or other tool, then insert the cuttings so they do not quite touch.

5 Firm the cuttings to make sure there are no large air pockets that would cause the cuttings or new roots to dry out.

6 Water the cuttings after planting, and keep an eye on them to make sure they do not dry out during the warm summer weather. It is worth adding a fungicide to the initial watering.

7 Label each row. By the time they root it is easy to forget what they are – especially if you take a lot of different summer cuttings.

Some Shrubs To Propagate

The following shrubs root easily from semi-ripe cuttings. But there are many others that will root successfully, so be prepared to experiment if your favourite shrub does not appear in the list.

Abelia
Buddleia (butterfly bush)
Camellia
Ceanothus (Californian lilac)
Chaenomeles (quince)
Choisya (Mexican orange blossom)
Cistus (sun rose)
Cotoneaster
Daphne
Deutzia
Elaeagnus
Escallonia
Euonymus
Forsythia
Fuchsia
Griselinia
Hebe
Helianthemum (rock rose)
Hibiscus
Hydrangea
Ligustrum (privet)
Philadelphus (mock orange)
Pieris
Potentilla
Pyracantha (firethorn)
Rhododendron
Ribes (flowering currant)
Rose
Rosemary
Santolina (cotton lavender)
Syringa (lilac)
Viburnum
Weigela

Santolina

Euonymus

Weigela

SPECIAL CUTTINGS

A few shrubs, such as clematis, sometimes root better if you use special techniques. These are some of the most useful methods.

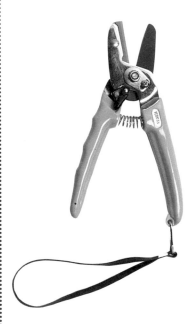

INTERNODAL CLEMATIS CUTTINGS

1 Take internodal cuttings to raise a lot of clematis rather than the smaller number achieved by layering. Remove a length of stem in the spring or early summer to cut into smaller sections.

2 Make each cutting by severing it from the stem *between* leaf joints (most cuttings are taken at a leaf joint or node). Leave about 2.5–5cm (1–2in) of stem below the leaves, with just a short stub of stem above the leaf joint.

3 Remove one of the two leaves, leaving a stump about 6mm (¼in) long. Leave the other leaf on as a convenient 'handle'.

4 Insert in the compost in the usual way. The cuttings will root more readily if you keep them in a propagator and maintain a humid atmosphere. Pot up the rooted plants individually and grow on for a season before planting out.

3 A long 'tail' is not needed to root the cutting, so trim it off close to the base of the cutting, using a sharp knife. Insert the cutting in compost as usual.

1 Some shrubs root better if the cutting is taken with a 'heel' of old wood – a slither of bark that remains when the cutting is pulled off. Evergreens such as rhododendrons and azaleas, and pieris, are among the shrubs that usually root more successfully if you take the cuttings with a heel. This method is also helpful for plants that have hollow stems, such as elders (*Sambucus*), and those with greenwood stems, such as brooms.

2 Remove the cutting by pulling downwards so that a piece of the main stem bark comes away with the cutting. The hormones that stimulate rooting are concentrated here.

4 Insert the trimmed cutting normally, in a cold frame, propagator or pot covered with a polythene bag. Use a rooting hormone on species that are slow to root.

RIGHT Juniperus cuttings usually root better if taken with a heel. Make them in early autumn.

ABOVE Cuttings are one of the ways that azaleas can be propagated, and some people like to take them with a heel.

LEFT Evergreen elaeagnus root readily from cuttings taken in late summer or early autumn. Leaving on a heel sometimes helps.

HARDWOOD CUTTINGS

Take hardwood cuttings in late autumn or when the shrubs are dormant. Most are easy to root and, because they are left in the ground rather than placed in pots, they need much less looking after than other types of cuttings.

TAKING HARDWOOD CUTTINGS

1 Choose shoots that grew during the summer but have now become firm and hard. Avoid very weak, thin shoots and those that are thick and old. Cut off the shoots with secateurs. They can be longer than the actual cuttings because you can take several from one shoot by dividing it into shorter lengths later.

2 Pull off any dying leaves that remain on the shoot, then cut it into sections about 15–23cm (6–9in) long.

3 So that you remember which end is the top, make a sloping cut just above the top bud, and a horizontal one at the appropriate distance underneath.

4 Choose a sheltered but not dry part of the garden to make a slit trench with a spade. Push the spade in vertically to the appropriate depth, then push it forwards to create an almost V-shaped trench.

5 To discourage water from standing around the base of the cuttings, which may cause rotting, sprinkle a thick layer of grit or coarse sand along the bottom of the trench before planting.

SINGLE STEM CUTTINGS

If you are taking cuttings of trees that you want to grow with a single stem, or fruit bushes with a single leg (stem), insert the cutting so the tip is just covered. This will discourage the growth of the lower buds on the stem.

6 For most shrubs, insert the cuttings so that only about 2.5–5cm (1–2in) shows above the ground. Insert vertically, about 10cm (4in) apart. Firm them in well.

Cornus alba and its varieties are grown mainly for their attractive coloured winter stems. They are very easy to propagate from hardwood cuttings.

ROOTING HORMONES

Rooting hormones – which can be powders or liquids – are most useful for plants that are difficult to root. They can be used on all stem cuttings, so you may prefer to use them routinely. However, they are not intended for use on leaf or root cuttings.

Most of the hormones will be taken up through the cut base of the cutting, not through the bark or stem, so you only need to dip the cut surface into the powder or liquid.

If using a powder, dip the tip of the cutting into water first, so the powder adheres to the cutting more readily.

Rooting hormones can be formulated with different chemicals and strengths to suit different types of cutting – such as hardwood or softwood – but most sold for amateurs are all-purpose.

Many contain a fungicide, which will reduce the risk of the cutting rotting before it has taken root.

Most rooting hormones used by amateurs come as powders.

Some hormones are dissolved in water or solvents, but those sold for amateurs are usually formulated as a gel.

PLANTS TO TRY

Most deciduous (leaf-shedding) shrubs can be propagated from hardwood cuttings. Popular ones that root easily from hardwood cuttings include:

Cotoneaster
Dogwood (*Cornus alba*)
Flowering currant (*Ribes sanguineum*)
Rose (below)
Winter-flowering viburnum

Trees can also be propagated from hardwood cuttings. Those that root readily include poplars (*Populus*) and willows (*Salix*).

LAYERING

Layering is an ideal way to propagate shrubs and some house plants if you need just a few extra plants. You will usually have a larger plant more quickly than you would from cuttings. Air layering is a good technique to use if you have a leggy plant that has become bare at the base. Simple layering is best for shrubs in the garden, but if you have a climber such as a clematis or honeysuckle you can use serpentine layering and root even more plants.

AFTERCARE

▪ Water thoroughly and try to prevent the soil drying out before the plant has rooted.
▪ Sever the stem from its parent in the autumn or spring (pull a little soil away with your hand to check whether the layer has rooted).
▪ After severing it from its parent, pinch out the growing tip of the new plant to make it bushy.
▪ Lift and replant if well-rooted; if not, leave for up to a year.

PLANTS TO TRY

Most shrubs and some trees can be layered if there are suitable low-growing shoots, but those that are often propagated this way include:
   Corylus avellana 'Contorta'
     (contorted willow)
   Hamamelis (witch hazel)
   Magnolia x *soulangeana*
   Magnolia stellata
   Rhododendron (opposite)
   Syringa vulgaris (lilac)
   Viburnum

SIMPLE LAYERING

1 Choose a young, low-growing branch flexible enough to be bent down easily, and trim the leaves and sideshoots off the part of the stem that will be in contact with the ground. Leave on some leaves at the end of the stem.

2 Lower the stem to the ground and note the point about 23cm (9in) behind the tip where it comes into contact with the soil. Then use a spade to make a hole 10–15cm (4–6in) deep that slopes towards the parent plant but has a vertical end.

3 Hold the stem in contact with the soil using a peg of bent wire or a forked stick. If you do not have suitable wire, try cutting a length from an old wire coat-hanger. Make sure that the end of the stem lies vertically against the back of the hole.

4 Return the excavated soil to bury the stem, and firm it in well (use the heel of your shoe if necessary).

AIR LAYERING

1 Trim off any leaves that are growing in the place where you want to make the layer. Make a polythene sleeve to go around the stem (you can use a polythene bag). Secure the bottom of the sleeve just below the layering point, which will be beneath an old leaf scar, using tape or a plastic-covered wire twist-tie.

2 Holding the sleeve out of the way, use a sharp knife or blade to make a slanting upward cut about 2.5cm (1in) long. Be careful not to cut more than half-way through the stem, or the shoot may break off completely.

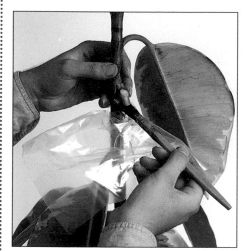

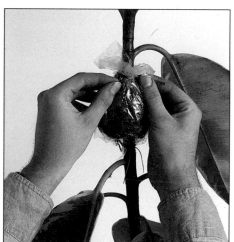

3 Brush a little hormone rooting powder or liquid into the cut, then pack with sphagnum moss to keep the wound open.

4 Pull the sleeve over the wounded area and pack it with plenty of moist sphagnum moss (try a florist if your garden centre does not have any). Secure at the top with more tape or another plastic-covered wire twist-tie.

AFTERCARE

■ Look after the parent plant normally and do not attempt to remove the layered section until you can see roots.

■ Once plenty of roots have formed, cut through the stem below the layered area. Loosen the ball of moss and tease out some of the roots when you pot it up.

PLANTS TO TRY

Air layering is most commonly used for indoor plants that have become bare at the base, but it can be used for garden trees and shrubs. Plants for which the technique is often used include:

Indoors
Ficus elastica (rubber plant)
Dracaena
Outdoors
Hamamelis (witch hazel)
Magnolia
Rhododendron (below)
Syringa (lilac)

SERPENTINE LAYERING

Strip the leaves from a healthy shoot at the points where the stem will be buried, leaving several intact so that the stem snakes in and out of the ground. At each joint, make a slanting cut about 2.5cm (1in) long and almost half-way through. Insert a small piece of matchstick in the cut to prevent it closing up again and pin down

with a piece of bent wire. Cover with soil, and keep well watered.
Plants to try Serpentine layering is suitable only for climbers or trailers with long stems that can be pegged to the ground, such as:
Clematis (opposite)
Lonicera, climbing forms (honeysuckle)
Parthenocissus (Boston ivy, Virginia creeper)

LEAF CUTTINGS

Leaf cuttings can be fun to root, and are an ideal way to propagate house plants such as African violets (*Saintpaulia*) and Cape primroses (*Streptocarpus*).

LEAF PETIOLE CUTTINGS

1 Plants such as African violets (*Saintpaulia*) can be propagated from leaf cuttings taken with the stalk (petiole) attached. Select young but fully-grown healthy leaves and cut them off cleanly.

2 Trim the stalk about 3cm (1¼in) below the leaf blade and insert in a pot of cuttings compost, vermiculite or perlite, so the bottom of the leaf blade is just in contact with the compost.

3 Cover with a mini cloche made from the upper section of a plastic drinks bottle, or use an inflated polythene bag held in place with an elastic band. Label and keep in a warm light place, out of direct sunlight.

4 Keep the compost damp but not wet, and remove any condensation from the cover regularly. Pot up the plantlet that grows from the base as soon as it is growing vigorously.

LEAF SECTION CUTTINGS

1 The leaves of the Cape primrose (*Streptocarpus*), and some other plants, can be cut into sections. Use a sharp knife or razor-blade to slice the leaves into sections 5–8cm (2–3in) wide.

2 Push each cut section vertically into a tray of cuttings compost. Keep the side that was nearest the leaf stalk downwards, and bury about one-third of the cutting.

3 Keep the compost just moist and in a warm light place, out of direct sunlight. When small plantlets grow at the base, pot them up individually.

African violets are particularly easy to root from leaf cuttings (see leaf petiole cuttings).

LEAF BLADE CUTTINGS

1 Some plants, such as *Begonia rex*, will produce new plants from the leaf blade (lamina). Choose mature but healthy leaves, and retain part of the stem. With a sharp knife, cut straight across the main veins from the underside, making each cut about 12mm (½in) long.

2 Place the leaf on a tray of compost, pushing the stub of the stalk in to help hold the leaf in position. Use a piece of bent wire to hold the veins in contact with the compost.

3 Alternatively, hold the leaf down with small stones.

4 Label, then keep the tray in a warm, light place, but out of direct sunlight. Once small plants have developed, carefully separate them from the leaf and pot up individually.

DIVISION

Division is one of the quickest and easiest methods of propagation, and ideal if you require just a few extra plants. Many herbaceous plants benefit from division anyway once they have formed a congested clump of growth after some years.

DIVIDING HERBACEOUS PLANTS

1 Divide large clumps as the shoots emerge in spring. Use a fork to loosen and lift the clump.

2 Use two forks back to back to tear the clump into smaller and more manageable pieces.

3 If you want just a couple of large plants, replant without further division, but discard any dead parts in the centre of the clump. To make more plants, pull the pieces into smaller segments. Some are too tough to pull apart with your hands, in which case cut through them with a knife or chop into smaller pieces with a spade.

4 Replant the small pieces into prepared ground. Rake in a balanced garden fertilizer before planting.

DIVIDING FLAG IRISES

1 Divide rhizomatous flag irises that have become congested after flowering. Lift the clump with a fork and shake off as much soil as possible.

2 You should replant the current season's growth, so cut away and discard the old part of the rhizome.

3 Trim the leaves to about 5–8cm (2–3in) from the rhizome. This will reduce the amount of water lost from the plant while new roots are growing.

DIVIDING AQUATIC PLANTS

1 If a planting basket has been used, the roots may have grown through it. Cut the roots flush with the basket, using a sharp knife, so that you can remove the plant. Use a spade to chop the clump into smaller pieces.

2 The roots of some plants, such as aquatic rushes and irises, are very tough, and it may be necessary to cut through them with a sharp knife. Replant the pieces in fresh compost, placing a new liner in the basket if using the old one.

DIVIDING BEGONIA TUBERS

1 Start the tubers off in late winter or early spring in trays of compost in a light, warm place. When you can see the shoots beginning to grow, cut the tubers into several pieces, making sure that each one has a shoot or bud.

2 Dust the cut surfaces with a fungicide, then pot up individually in small pots.

DIVIDING DAHLIA TUBERS

If you require only two or three extra dahlia plants from your tuber, division is an alternative to cuttings. In late spring divide the tubers into two or three smaller clumps with a sharp knife. Always make sure that each piece has some shoots starting to grow, or buds. Ensure that there is a piece of old stem attached – isolated tubers will not grow. Alternatively, start the tubers off in boxes or trays. When the growth is a few centimetres high, cut through the tuber, making sure that each piece has a shoot. Dust cut surfaces with a fungicide then pot up until it is safe to plant outside.

4 Replant on a slight ridge of soil, spreading the roots either side. Cover the roots with soil, but leave the top of the rhizome exposed.

ROOT CUTTINGS

Root cuttings are usually taken in winter when there is not much outdoor propagation to be done. Several border plants and alpines root readily with this technique, which is an interesting propagation method to add to your repertoire.

TAKING ROOT CUTTINGS

1 Lift the parent plant with a fork to expose the roots, or scrape away enough soil to gain access to the roots without lifting the plant completely.

2 If the plant has thick, fleshy roots, cut some off with secateurs or a pruning knife, close to the main stem or root.

3 Cut each root into 5cm (2in) lengths. To enable you to remember which way up to plant the roots, cut them horizontally across the top, but make a sloping cut at the bottom end.

4 Insert the cuttings into pots of a gritty compost (such as a loam-based potting compost with extra grit added). The top of the cuttings should be flush with the top of the compost.

5 Sprinkle a thin layer of grit over the surface, and don't forget to insert a label, as nothing will be visible until the plants root a few months later. Keep in a cold frame or cool greenhouse.

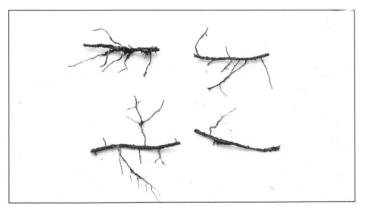

6 Some plants, such as perennial phlox, do not have thick, fleshy roots. In that case cut the finer roots into 5–8cm (2–3in) lengths, and do not worry about making horizontal or sloping cuts.

7 Lay the cuttings flat on the compost in a seed tray, then cover with compost.

PLANTS TO TRY

Root cuttings should always be taken when the plant is dormant – preferably in early winter.

Border perennials to try include acanthus, echinops, gaillardias, gypsophila, Oriental poppies (*Papaver orientale*), and border phlox.

Some alpines, such as the pasque flower (*Pulsatilla vulgaris*), can also be raised from root cuttings, as well as a few trees.

Romneya coulteri is an imposing shrub with flowers about 10cm (4in) across on a plant about 1.2–1.8m (4–6ft) tall. It can be propagated from 7.5cm (3in) root cuttings taken in mid winter.

PRUNING 1

Most shrubs require minimal pruning other than to remove dead or diseased shoots, but for some shrubs pruning will encourage better-flowering or more compact plants. The advice applies only to shrubs that have been established for at least a couple of years. Young plants may not require such severe pruning.

PRUNING FOR COLOURED STEMS

1 Dogwoods (*Cornus alba* and *Cornus stolonifera* varieties) and *Salix alba* 'Chermesina' (syn. 'Britzensis') should be pruned annually or every second year to encourage bright young stems like the ones shown here.

2 Prune in early spring, before the new leaves appear. Cut back each stem to an outward-facing bud about 5cm (2in) from the stump of hard wood.

3 The pruning will look severe when the shrub is cut back to a framework perhaps only 30cm (12in) high, but new shoots will soon appear.

PRUNING GREY-LEAVED SHRUBS

1 Small grey-leaved plants such as cotton lavender (*Santolina chamaecyparissus*) and the curry plant (*Helichrysum angustifolium*) need regular pruning to prevent them becoming straggly. Prune annually in the spring.

2 Cut back close to the base, to a point where new shoots can be seen. This may be as low as 10cm (4in) from the ground on plants pruned regularly, but to a taller framework of woody shoots on a neglected plant.

3 After pruning the plant will look like this, but new shoots will soon grow and by summer will make a compact, well-clothed shrub.

PRUNING THE WHITEWASH BRAMBLE

1 A few shrubs, such as *Rubus cockburnianus*, the whitewash bramble, are grown for their decorative winter stems that arise directly from the ground like raspberry canes. Prune these annually in late winter or early spring.

2 Pruning is very simple. Just cut all the stems off close to the ground. If the plant is very prickly, like this whitewash bramble, wear gloves for protection.

3 The pruning looks drastic, but new shoots will soon grow, and these will be more attractive the following winter than if you had left the old canes on the plant.

PRUNING HEATHERS

1 Prune heathers by clipping them with shears to remove the dead flowerheads. This will keep the plants compact as well as looking neater.

2 Trim the shoots back after flowering, close to the base of the current year's growth. Prune winter-flowering heathers in spring, and cut close to the base of the previous year's growth. Be careful not to cut into old, hardened wood.

Heathers become woody with age, with less compact growth and poor flowering. Keep their shape by clipping the dead heads off with shears after flowering.

PRUNING 2

Many shrubs, such as buddleias, need pruning every year. Others, such as brooms, will be better for a good prune. Slow-growing compact plants like cistus don't have to be pruned routinely at all, but it will stimulate the growth of more sideshoots and therefore more flowers the following year.

PRUNING DECIDUOUS SUCKERING SHRUBS

Deciduous suckering shrubs, such as *Kerria japonica* and *Leycesteria formosa*, will be a better shape and won't become too congested if you prune them every spring. Prune the flowered stems back to about half their original length, to a point where there is a strong sideshoot. Wait until flowering has finished if it's a spring-flowering shrub like kerria.

Remove about one-third of all the stems to within 5–8cm (2–3in) of the ground. Choose the oldest or weakest, or diseased or damaged shoots, to cut back hard.

PRUNING TO A FRAMEWORK

1 Plants that flowered the previous year, from mid summer onwards, *on shoots produced that year*, like this buddleia, need pruning every spring to keep them compact. All the growth on this plant was made after hard pruning the previous spring.

2 Cut back all the shoots each spring to within about two buds of the previous year's growth from the old stump. Long-handled pruners are best for this job.

3 This is what the plant will look like after pruning. It seems drastic, but the new shoots will grow rapidly and flower later in the year.

REDUCING NEW GROWTH BY HALF

1 Some shrubs, such as broom (Cytisus) and genista, still flower well if you don't prune them, but they become tall and straggly, with a bare base. You can tidy them up after flowering and prune to keep the plants compact at the same time. But you need to start when the plants are still young – you can't do much about a shrub that has already become bare and woody at the base.

2 Prune back all the new green shoots by about half the length of the light green growth. *Do not cut back into old, dark wood that has become hard.*

PRUNING SLOW-GROWING SUMMER-FLOWERING SHRUBS

1 Slow-growing and naturally compact summer-flowering shrubs, such as sun roses (cistus) and *Convolvulus cneorum*, that flower on sideshoots produced the previous year, grow well without pruning. But you can keep them shapely and stimulate more sideshoots and flowers by pruning as soon as flowering has finished.

2 Cut back the new growth – which is soft and pale – by about two-thirds. Always cut to just above a leaf joint or to a point where there is a young shoot.

PRUNING 3

Climbers sometimes need careful pruning to restrict their height and spread, and to keep them flowering well towards the base.

PRUNING A RAMBLER ROSE

1 In late summer, after flowering, cut out any very old, dead or diseased shoots right to the base, using long-handled pruners. Do not cut back the younger, healthy shoots.

2 Go along each of the remaining main shoots in turn and prune all the sideshoots from these to between two and four pairs of leaves from the main stem.

PRUNING A CLIMBING ROSE

1 In late summer or the autumn, cut out any dead, diseased or damaged shoots. If there are very old main stems, cut one or two of these back to the base of the plant.

2 On old climbers, cut one or two of the thick shoots back to about 30cm (12in) above the ground to encourage new shoots to grow from the base.

3 Work along each of the remaining main shoots in turn and reduce the length of all the sideshoots from each of them to about 15cm (6in).

Pruning Clematis

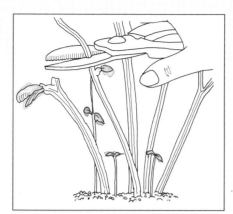

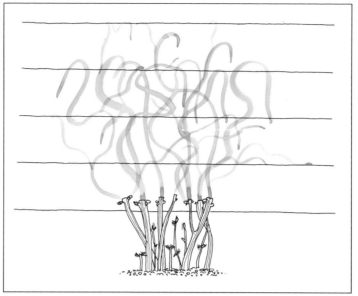

1 If your clematis flowers from mid or late summer, on growth produced in the current year, prune severely in late winter or early spring, before new growth commences. Prune all the stems back to a pair of leaf buds just above the previous year's growth – about 15–30cm (6–12in) above the ground.

2 This is what the plant will look like after pruning. Although the pruning seems severe, the new shoots produced will flower prolifically later in the year.

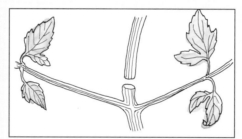

3 If your clematis flowers in early to mid summer on shoots that grow from the previous season's main stems, possibly with another flush of flowers in autumn, you must prune more selectively. Before new growth starts in early spring, cut back about a third of the stems to about 30cm (12in) above the ground, and also remove any dead or diseased shoots.

4 To restrict the size of the plant and encourage more flowering sideshoots, shorten the remaining long branches to a strong pair of buds.

5 If your clematis has relatively small flowers and blooms in spring or early summer, such as *C. montana*, prune only to restrict the size if it becomes too large. Immediately after flowering, thin or remove stems that are diseased, dead or causing overcrowding. Cut them right back to their point of origin.

RIGHT Most clematis that flower on old wood require minimal or moderate pruning, but those that flower on growth produced in the current year will become bare of flowers at the base unless pruned annually.

RUSTIC ARCHES AND PERGOLAS

An arch or pergola made from rustic timber is relatively simple to construct and is sure to look good with climbing plants. Leave the bark on or use peeled wood: it doesn't matter. If the bark is stripped there will be fewer hiding places for insects, however, and the wood is easier to work with.

Rustic poles can be used to make an attractive support for climbing and rambling roses, as well as arches and pergolas. The same basic joints are used.

A RUSTIC PERGOLA

1 A pergola must also be made to dimensions and designs that suit your garden, so plan it on paper first.

2 The easiest way to fix the horizontal poles to the uprights is to make a notch in the top of each upright that will take the horizontal snugly.

3 For a long pergola it will be necessary to join poles. Saw two opposing and matching notches as shown. Make sure that the joint occurs over an upright pole to support it. Like all the joints, fix firmly with rustproof nails.

4 Notch the cross-pieces by sawing a V-shape first, and adjusting it with a chisel if necessary. Nail into place with rustproof nails.

BELOW Clematis are often grown against a wall, but try growing them over an arch.

1 Sketch your design on paper before cutting any timber. A basic design is shown here, but modify it to suit the situation and height and width required.

Remember that you need to allow about 60cm (2ft) extra on the uprights to sink into the ground.

2 Assemble the pieces to your own design using a series of basic joints. This is a convenient and strong way to fix horizontals to uprights.

3 Where two pieces cross, mark the position and cut halving joints in each one. Use a saw and chisel to remove the section of timber.

4 You can use a wood glue for additional strength, but you will also need to hold each joint with a rustproof nail.

5 Bird's mouth joints are useful for connecting some of the pieces, especially horizontal or diagonal pieces to uprights. Mark the position carefully, then cut out a V-shape about 2.5cm (1in) deep. Saw the other piece to fit – some trial and error is inevitable. Drive a nail diagonally through the joint.

6 Assemble the sides on the ground first, then make the top separately. Insert the uprights in prepared holes and hold them in position temporarily with wooden struts. Drill and then screw the top into position. Nailing may not be stable enough for this position, and it may put strain on the structure before the uprights have properly settled in.

FENCES

Every garden has a boundary, and unless it's secure your garden is at risk. Walls and fences do more than just keep people and animals in or out of your garden, however, they can look attractive and can provide those vertical spaces so useful if you like climbing plants.

ERECTING A PANEL FENCE

1 Panel fences are easy to erect, and if you use post spikes you will save the effort of digging holes and setting the posts in concrete. Just buy a special tool to protect the top, then drive them in with a sledge-hammer.

2 It is essential that the spikes are driven in absolutely vertically, so keep checking with a spirit-level.

3 Once a post spike has been driven in, insert the post itself, and again check that it is vertical.

4 Lay the panel in position on the ground, to mark the point for the next post spike.

5 Drive the next spike in, and check that the post is vertical. Do not leave the post in position yet, otherwise you will find it difficult to insert the panel.

6 Panel brackets are the easiest way to fix the panels to the posts. Nail the brackets to the post already in position, and at the appropriate height on the next post to be erected.

7 Insert the panel, and while someone holds it in position erect the next post to hold it there. Then nail through the brackets into the panel to hold it firm.

8 Check both before and after nailing through the brackets that the panel is absolutely horizontal.

9 Finish off by nailing a post cap to the top of each post. This will prevent water soaking the top of the post and extend the life of the timber.

RIGHT Although panel fences are quick and easy to erect, there are plenty of other fence designs to try. Here, vertical boards have been nailed either side of the horizontal bars so that they overlap slightly.

WALLS

Tall boundary walls do not make a good DIY project unless you already have bricklaying experience. You will also have to consider strengthening piers for safety. A low garden wall like the one illustrated is suitable as an internal divider as well as a low boundary, and makes a simple bricklaying job with which to start.

MORTAR AND CONCRETE MIXES

For footings (wall foundations), and the foundation for a drive or pre-cast paving
1 part cement
2½ parts sharp sand*
3½ parts 2cm (¾in) aggregate*
*Instead of using separate aggregate and sand, you can use 5 parts of combined aggregate to every 1 part cement.

Bedding mortar (to bed and joint concrete or brick paving)
1 part cement
5 parts sharp sand

Masonry mortar (for brickwork)
1 part cement
3 parts soft sand

All parts are by volume and not weight. In hot climates, setting retardants may be necessary; in cold climates, a kind of antifreeze may have to be added. If in doubt, ask your builder's merchant for more specific advice.

BUILDING A LOW BRICK WALL

1 Even a low wall requires a footing (foundation). Excavate a trench about 30cm (12in) deep and place 13cm (5in) of consolidated hardcore in the base. Drive in pegs as a guide for levelling the concrete. Check the level between the pegs at this stage.

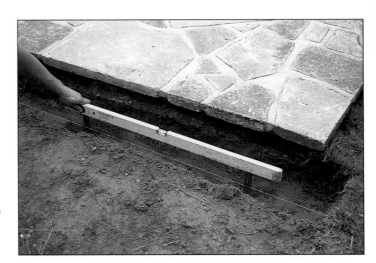

2 Pour in the concrete, and level it off with the pegs. Use a piece of wood to tamp the concrete level and to remove large pockets of air.

3 Leave the concrete to harden for a few days, then lay the first course of bricks. It is important to form a small pier at each end – and at intervals along the wall if it's a long one – as shown.

4 Continue to lay subsequent courses, first laying a ribbon of mortar on top of the previous row, and 'buttering' one end of each brick to be laid, as shown.

5 Use a spirit level frequently, and strike off any surplus mortar from the sides of the wall as you work.

6 Use the handle of the bricklaying trowel to firm and adjust the level of each brick as you lay it.

7 Finish off the wall with coping, and pier caps. This will make the wall look more attractive and also protect the brickwork from excessive moisture.

Bricks are a 'sympathetic' building material for paths and walls, and they can often help to integrate house and garden particularly effectively. A raised bed like this is a straightforward project to try, even if you have no previous bricklaying experience.

SURFACES AND PATHS 1

Along with the lawn, hard surfaces such as paving create the backbone of the garden. Plants add the shape and form, but paving has a profound effect on the visual impact of a garden, so it's important to take care to get it looking good.

LAYING PAVING SLABS

1 Whether it is a path or patio that you are laying, try to prepare a proper foundation. The depth of hardcore (rubble) needed will depend on the weight the paving has to support: about 5–10cm (2–4in) of hardcore is plenty for foot traffic, but if it has to take vehicles, increase it to about 15cm (6in). Remove the earth to an appropriate depth, allowing for the hardcore and the thickness of mortar and slab.

2 Compact the ground. You might be able to do this by treading it and banging it with a suitable improvised tamping tool, but a flat-plate vibrator like this is worth considering for a large area (you can hire one).

3 Add the hardcore, and check the approximate depth by using a straight-edge across the area and a steel rule.

4 Compact the hardcore by tamping it or hitting it with a club or sledge-hammer (this will also help to break large pieces).

5 Bed the slabs on five blobs of mortar – one just in from each corner and one in the centre. A mixture of 1 part cement to 5 parts sharp sand is suitable for most slab-laying jobs.

6 Place the slab in position, positioning it as accurately as possible, and lowering it down from one side.

7 Tap it into position with the handle of a hammer or mallet, using a spirit-level to make sure that the surface is even. If you are laying a large area of paving it will be necessary to lay it with a slight slope so that rainwater drains away freely.

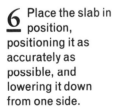

GARDENING BASICS

84

8 Do not rely on using the spirit-level across just a pair of slabs. Angle it across other nearby slabs too, to ensure that it is level in all directions.

9 Some paving slabs are designed to fit with flush joints, but others are intended for mortared joints. Use home-made spacers to ensure a consistent gap for the mortar.

10 Fill the joints with a small pointing trowel. The effect usually looks crisper if the mortar is slightly recessed.

LAYING BRICK PAVING

1 The method shown here uses bricks bedded on mortar, but you can achieve a very similar effect (except for the mortar joints) by bedding clay pavers on sand. To lay bricks on mortar, prepare the base as described for paving slabs, but spread an even layer of mortar over the area being laid. If you lay the sides of a path first, it will be easier to check levels.

2 Lay several rows of bricks in your chosen pattern, pressing them gently into the bed of mortar. Then pass a piece of wood across the width of the path and tamp down with the handle of a hammer or mallet, to ensure that they are all level.

3 The easiest way to mortar the joints is to brush a dry mortar mix into the gaps between the bricks. Press down between the edges with a small piece of wood occasionally to make sure that there are no large air pockets.

4 Water gently from a watering-can fitted with a rose. Do not flood the area. Apply just enough water to clean the surface of the bricks and moisten between the joints. If necessary, clean any mortar stains off the surface of the bricks with a damp cloth before it dries.

RIGHT Bricks and plants look good together, as these petunias tumbling over the edge of a low brick edging testify.

SURFACES AND PATHS 2

Paths and other hard surface areas can be the dominant part of the garden design, so give as much thought to these as to the plantings that will eventually soften any of the hard outlines. Be prepared to mix materials, and to use different surfaces together: the stepping-stone path picture opposite makes an imposing focal point yet has the practical function of protecting the lawn too.

LAYING PAVERS

1 Clay pavers look like bricks but are thinner and are designed to fit together without mortar joints. Concrete pavers are designed in a similar way and are laid using the same technique.

After preparing a sub-base of about 5–10cm (2–4in) of compacted hardcore, mortar into position a firm edge to work from. You can buy special edging to match the pavers or use concrete edging like this. Check levels and adjust if necessary.

2 Lay a 5cm (2in) deep bed of sand. Make sure that the pavers will be level with the edging when laid on the sand. Adjust the depth of the sand layer if necessary. Use battens as a height gauge and to enable the sand to be levelled with a third piece of wood.

3 Lay the pavers in the required pattern, making sure that they butt up to each other and to the edging.

4 Use a flat-plate vibrator (which you can hire) to settle the pavers into the sand. If you can't obtain a flat-plate vibrator, tamp the pavers down with a club hammer used over a length of timber.

5 Brush more sand over the pavers, so that it fills the joints. Then vibrate or tamp again. It may be necessary to brush further sand over the paving, and vibrate again, to lock the pavers firmly into position.

LAYING STEPPINGSTONES

1 So that stepping-stones are comfortable to walk on, pace out the area to indicate where each one should be when you walk with a normal stride.

2 Lay the stones on the lawn, then stand back to make sure they look right visually. This is especially important if you want the stepping-stones to form a curved path.

3 Walk over the stones once more before you set them into the lawn, to make sure that the spacing feels right to walk on.

A stepping-stone path like this can take the eye across to another focal point or vista, as well as saving wear and tear on the lawn. In wet weather it will also protect your shoes.

4 Cut around the edge of each stone with a spade (or a half-moon edger if you have one), deep enough to be able to remove a slice of grass a little deeper than the stepping-stone.

5 Slice beneath the grass with a spade, then lift out the piece of turf. It does not matter if you dig a little too deeply as the layer of sand will even out irregularities.

6 Use a little sand to level the base and bring the stepping-stone to the right height. Make sure it is level and set just below the surrounding grass (if set too high it could damage the mower).

SURFACES AND PATHS 3

A large area of plain paving – whether bricks or slabs – can look boring. Think about creating a more interesting effect by mixing paving materials. And if you have a path to lay, a crazy-paving style might give your garden the kind of old-fashioned charm that it needs, especially if you choose natural stone or a sympathetic substitute.

LAYING CRAZY PAVING

1 Always lay the pieces dry first, concentrating on the large pieces and making sure those with reasonably straight edges go at the sides. You can fill in with smaller pieces once the key pieces have been arranged.

2 When the pieces have been arranged loosely, start to bed them on a mortar mix (1 part cement to 5 parts sharp sand is suitable). Use a spirit-level to keep the path as level as possible.

3 Use a piece of board across the width of the paving to help create a level finish. Tamp individual pieces of paving with the handle of a hammer or mallet if necessary.

4 Finish off by mortaring between the joints, using a small pointing trowel. You can add a cement dye if you wish to create a matching or contrasting colour for the joints.

MIXING MATERIALS

Do not be afraid to mix materials: railway sleepers and bricks or clay pavers look good together, gravel helps to soften the harsh effect of rectangular paving slabs, and rows of bricks can be used very effectively to break up a large expanse of concrete paving slabs.

RIGHT Combine pavers with a range of different pebbles to create an interesting surface.

INTRODUCING PEBBLES

1 Beach pebbles can be used to make a paved path more interesting, or as a device to absorb some of the gaps created when you have to lay a curved path with rectangular slabs. First create a bed of mortar, then lay the stones as closely together as you can.

2 Use a stout piece of wood, laid across the adjoining slabs, to ensure that the tops of the pebbles are flush with the paving (which will ensure they are reasonably comfortable to walk on). Tap the wood down with a hammer if necessary to bed them in evenly.

EDGINGS

A smart edge will put that finishing touch to a path, bed or border . . . and will prevent undue wear at the edge of a lawn.

1 Excavate a shallow trench deep enough to accommodate the edging. This comes in various sizes and designs – the design being laid in these pictures is known as a rope pattern.

2 It is essential that the edging can be laid flush with the path, so chisel off any mortar or rubble that protrudes beneath the path.

3 Gently tap each piece down with the handle of a hammer, using the eye initially to make sure they are level.

4 Back fill with soil, then compact it to ensure that each piece is stable. Add more soil and compact again until the edging is firm.

5 Use a long spirit level to ensure that the edging is straight. Small adjustments can be made by tapping with the handle of a hammer, but for large edgings you may have to add or remove soil.

FIXING A WOODEN EDGE

1 Unwind the roll, and if it is too long cut it to size. Use wire-cutters or strong pliers to snip through the strands of wire.

2 Decide on the height above the ground that you want the top, then excavate a trench of appropriate depth. This type of edging is useful if you want to create a low raised bed to fill with soil later.

3 If you need to join pieces, lay them in position then wire together. Make sure the edging is at the appropriate height, and reasonably level, then back fill with soil and compact it.

4 Lay a long piece of wood with a straight edge over the top of the edging, and use a club hammer on this to knock it firmly into place and ensure that the top is level.

LAYING A LAWN EDGING STRIP

1 Use a spade to form a slit trench along the edge of the lawn. Keep the back of the slit as vertical as possible.

2 Unroll the edging strip and cut it to the appropriate length. Lay it loosely in the trench to help judge this.

3 Back fill with soil, firming it without pressing so hard that you distort the shape of the edging.

4 Finish off by tapping it level with the handle of a hammer over a straight-edged piece of wood. Make sure that the edging does not stand above lawn level, otherwise the mower may be damaged.

A brick edging gives a smart finish to a path or lawn.

SUPPLIERS

UK

GARDEN EQUIPMENT AND SUPPLIES

Axminster Power Tool Centre
Chard Street
Axminster
Devon EX13 5DZ
Tel: 01297 33656
Fax: 01297 35242

Greevale Farm Ltd
(Fisons Origins Range)
Wonastow Road
Monmouth
Gwent NP5 3XX

Humber Fertilizers
PO Box 27
Stoneferry
Hull
Humberside HU8 8DQ

Jemp Engineering Ltd
(soil warming cable)
Canal Estate
Station Road
Langley
Berkshire SL3 6EG

P G Horticulture
(modules)
Street Farm
Thornham Magna
Eye
Suffolk IP23 8HB

SEEDS

B & T World Seeds
Whitenell House
Fiddington
Bridgwater
Somerset TA5 1JE

D T Brown & Co Ltd
Station Road
Poulton-le-Fylde
Blackpool
Lancashire FY6 7HX
Tel: 01253 882371

Chiltern Seeds
Bortree Stile
Ulverston
Cumbria LA12 7PB
Tel: 01229 581137

Cowcombe Farm Herbs
Gipsy Lane
Chalford
Stroud
Gloucestershire GL6 8HP

Samuel Dobie & Sons Ltd
Broomhill Way
Torquay
Devon TQ2 7QW
Tel: 01803 616281

King Crown Quality Seeds
Monks Farm
Pantling Lane
Coggleshall Road
Kelvedon
Essex CO5 9PG

Seeds by Size
70 Varney Road
Hemel Hempstead
Hertfordshire HP1 1TB

Seymour's Selected Seeds
Abacus House
Station Yard
Needham Market
Suffolk IP6 8AS

Stewart's (Nottingham) Ltd
3 George Street
Nottingham
NG1 3BH
Tel: 0115 976338

PONDS AND FOUNTAINS

J N S
21 Greenside
Prestwood
Buckinghamshire HP16 0SE

Pondliners
Freepost 62
Nicolson Link
Clifton Moor
York YO1 1SS
Tel: 01904 691169
Fax: 01904 691133

Reef Aquatics
Catfoot Lane
Lambley
Nottinghamshire NG4 4QG
Tel: 0115 976100
Fax: 0115 973266

Stapeley Water Gardens Ltd
London Road
Nantwich
Cheshire
Tel: 01270 628111

The Very Interesting Rock Company
PO Box 27
Leamington Spa
Warwickshire CV32 5GR
Tel: 01926 313465

GREENHOUSES, SUNROOMS AND CONSERVATORIES

Alispeed Ltd
Unit B4
Hortonwood 10
Telford
Shropshire TF1 4ES

Alite Metals
7 Maze Street
Barton Hill
Bristol BS5 9TE
Tel: 0117 953100

Archwood Greenhouses
Robinwood
Goodrich
Herefordshire HR9 6HT
Tel: 01600 890125

Regal National Garden Building Centre
Cromford Road
Langley Mill
Nottinghamshire NG16 4EB
Tel: 01773 530428

GARDEN STRUCTURES AND ORNAMENTS

Agriframes Ltd
Charlwoods Road
East Grinstead
W Sussex RH19 2HG

Capital Garden Products Ltd
Hurst Green
Etchingham
E Sussex TN19 7QU
Tel: 01580 201092

FENCING

Lemar
Harrowbrook Industrial Estate
Hinckley
Leicestershire LE10 3DJ
Tel: 01455 637077

M C Products
Home Farm Cliffe
Piercebridge
Darlington
Co Durham DL2 3SS

Rob Turner
Unit 16
Moore's Yard
High Street
Stalham
Norfolk NR12 9AN
Tel: 01692 580091

AUSTRALIA

GARDEN CENTRES

Swanes
490 Galston Road
Dural NSW 2158
Tel: (02) 651 1322
Fax: (02) 651 2146

**Michele Shennen's
Garden Centres**
44 Old Barrenjoey Road
Avalon NSW 2107
Tel: (02) 918 6738

Rast Brothers
29 Kissing Point Road
Turramurra NSW 2074
Tel: (02) 44 2134

Tropigro
PO Box 39827
Winnellie NT 0821
Tel: (089) 84 3200
Fax: (089) 47 0448

Gardenway Nurseries
269 Monier Road
Darra QLD 4076

Perrots Nursery
71 Elkhorn Street
Enoggera QLD 4051
Tel: (07) 355 7700

Gippsland Growers
125 Sutton Street
Warragul VIC 3920
Tel/Fax: (056) 23 6718

Warner's Nurseries Pty Ltd
395 Warrigal Road
Burwood VIC 3125
Tel: (03) 808 2321
Fax: (03) 808 5983

Wattleview Gardens
32 Wattletree Road
Ferntree Gully VIC 3156
Tel: (03) 758 6449

Richgro Horticultural Products
Lot 186 Acourt Road
Canningvale WA 6155
Tel: (09) 455 1323
Fax: (09) 455 1297

SEEDS

Australian Seed Company
(Australian native tree and shrub seeds)
5 Rosedale Avenue
Hazelbrook NSW 2779
Tel: (047) 58 6132

Ellison Horticultural
(tree, shrub and palm seeds)
PO Box 365
Nowra NSW 2541
Tel: (044) 21 4255
Fax: (044) 23 0859

Harvest Seed Company
(wholesale native and exotic seed &
seedling suppliers)
PO Box 544
Newport Beach NSW 2106
Tel: (02) 997 2277
Fax: (02) 997 6924

Diggers Seeds
Box 300
Dromana VIC 3936
Tel: (059) 871877

NEW ZEALAND

NURSERIES

Big Trees
Main Road
Coatesville
Auckland
Tel: (09) 415-9983

Golden Coast Nurseries
Main Road
North Paekakariki
Tel: 292-8556
Fax: 292-8556

Kent's Nurseries
Cr. Fergusson Drive & Ranfurly Street
Trentham
Tel: (4) 528-3889

Rainbow Tree Nursery
Cooper Road
Ramarama
Sth. Auckland

GARDENING CENTRES

California Green World Garden Centre
139 Park Road
Miramar
Wellington
Tel: (04) 388-3260
Fax: (04) 388-4820

Palmers Garden World
Cr. Shore & Orakei Roads
Remuera
Auckland
Tel: (09) 524 4038

Plantarama Garden Centre
104 State Highway 16
Massy
Auckland

Zeniths
92 Epuni Street
Lower Hutt
Tel: (04) 566-1493

GARDEN POOL CENTRES

Garden Statues and Ornaments
Hewletts Road
Mt Maunganui
Tel: (07) 575-5797
Fax: (07) 552-5244

Jansen's Pet Centre
985 Mt Eden Road
Three Kings
Auckland
Tel: (09) 625-7915

STATUARY

Ornamentally Yours
12 Princess Street
Onehunga
Auckland
Tel: (09) 634-4305
Fax: (09) 622-1029

Garden Statues and Ornaments
(see Garden Pool Centres)

GAZEBOS

Wellington Sheds & Carports
Cr. Petone Esplanade & Hutt Road
Petone
Wellington
Tel: (04) 568-9626

INDEX

Page numbers in italic refer to the illustrations

A

African violets: from leaf cuttings 66, 67
air layering 64, 65
alpines: propagating 70, 71
    sowing 46–7, 52
aphids 40
aquatic plants, dividing 69
arches, rustic 79
aubretia: from seed 52
azaleas, propagating 61, 61

B

bedding plants: pricking out 48
    sowing 46–7
begonias: dividing tubers 69
    taking leaf blade cuttings 67
biennials, sowing 53
blackfly 40, 40
blackleg 44, 44
blood, dried 32, 32
blood, fish and bonemeal 32, 32
bonemeal 32, 32
brambles, whitewash: pruning 73, 73
brick paving, laying 85, 85

brick walls, building 82–3
broom: pruning 75, 75
    taking heel cuttings 61
buddleia: pruning 74, 74
    from semi–ripe cuttings 58–9
bulbs, storing 44

C

cabbages: and club-root 44
Cape primroses: from cuttings 66, 66
carrot fly 42
caterpillars 41
chrysanthemums: from cuttings 57, 57
cistus: propagating 59
    pruning 74, 75
clay soil: draining 26–7
    improving 27
    liming 25, 27
    testing for 25
clematis: growing on an arch 78, 78
    layering 64, 65
    pruning 77, 77
    taking internodal cuttings 60, 60
climbers: layering 64, 65
    pruning 76
club-root 44
cold damage 45, 45
compost 32
    constructing bin for 28, 28
    digging in 27, 27
    making 29, 29
concrete mixes 82
Cornus alba see dogwood
cotoneaster, propagating 59, 63
cotton lavender, pruning 72, 72
crazy paving, laying 88, 88
cucumbers: pricking out 49
    root diseases 44
cultivators, hand 13, 13, 23, 36
cuttings: basal stem 56–7
    greenwood 55
    hardwood 62–3
    heel 61
    internodal 60
    leaf 66–7
    root 70–1
    semi-ripe 58, 59
    single stem 62
    softwood 54
cutworms 42

D

dahlias: dividing tubers 69
    pricking out 49
    taking cuttings 57
daisy grubbers 12, 13
deciduous shrubs, propagating 62–3
delphinium cuttings, taking 56, 56

Digging

digging (*see also* spades) 20–1, *20–1*
    for fine tilth 22, 22
diseases *see* pests and diseases
division 68–9
dogwood (*Cornus alba*): pruning 72
    taking cuttings 62, 63, 63

downy mildew 43, 43
draining soil 26–7, 26–7
drip feed systems 34

E

earwigs 41
edgings: brick 91, 91
    for lawns 19, 91, 91
    terracotta 90, 90
    wooden 90, 90
edging tools 19, 19
elaeagnus: from cuttings 59, 61
Encarsia formosa (wasp) 40
evergreen shrubs: taking heel cuttings 61

F

fasciated stems 45, 45
fences, panel 80–1, 80–1
fertilizers: applying 30, 30
    inorganic 31
    and lime applications 25
    organic 32, 32, 33
    see also green manuring
fish meal 32, 33
flowering currant: taking cuttings 59, 63
foot and root rots 44
forks 12, 12, 13
    using 21
fuchsias: taking cuttings 54
fungus leaf diseases 43